BOOK ONE

The Take-Action Guide to

World Class

Learners

This book is dedicated to helping schools and teachers to transform their educational setting into a global campus so as to enable the development of globally competent entrepreneurs.

BOOK ONE

The Take-Action Guide to
World Class
Learners

Personalized Education
for Autonomous Learning
and Student-Driven Curriculum

Yong Zhao
Homa Tavangar • Emily McCarren,
Gabriel F. Rshaid • and Kay Tucker

CORWIN
A SAGE Company

FOR INFORMATION:

Corwin

A SAGE Company

2455 Teller Road

Thousand Oaks, California 91320

(800) 233-9936

www.corwin.com

SAGE Publications Ltd.

1 Oliver's Yard

55 City Road

London EC1Y 1SP

United Kingdom

SAGE Publications India Pvt. Ltd.

B 1/I 1 Mohan Cooperative Industrial Area

Mathura Road, New Delhi 110 044

India

SAGE Publications Asia-Pacific Pte. Ltd.

3 Church Street

#10-04 Samsung Hub

Singapore 049483

Printed in the United States of America

ISBN 978-1-4833-3948-1

This book is printed on acid-free paper.

Executive Editor: Arnis Burvikovs

Associate Editor: Desirée A. Bartlett

Editorial Assistant: Andrew Olson

Production Editor: Amy Schroller

Copy Editor: Christina West

Typesetter: C&M Digitals (P) Ltd.

Proofreader: Laura Webb

Indexer: Rick Hurd

Cover Designer: Rose Storey

Marketing Manager: Amy Vader

Certified Chain of Custody
Promoting Sustainable Forestry
www.sfiprogram.org
SFI-01268

SFI label applies to text stock

15 16 17 18 19 10 9 8 7 6 5 4 3 2 1

DISCLAIMER: This book may direct you to access third-party content via Web links, QR codes, or other scannable technologies, which are provided for your reference by the author(s). Corwin makes no guarantee that such third-party content will be available for your use and encourages you to review the terms and conditions of such third-party content. Corwin takes no responsibility and assumes no liability for your use of any third-party content, nor does Corwin approve, sponsor, endorse, verify, or certify such third-party content.

Contents

About the
Authors

 Yong Zhao currently serves as the Presidential Chair and Director of the Institute for Global and Online Education in the College of Education, University of Oregon, where he is also a Professor in the Department of Educational Measurement, Policy, and Leadership. He is also a professorial fellow at the Mitchell Institute for Health and Education Policy, Victoria University. His works focus on the implications of globalization and technology on education. He has published over 100 articles and 20 books, including *Who's Afraid of the Big Bad Dragon?: Why China Has the Best (and Worst) Education System in the World*, *Catching Up or Leading the Way: American Education in the Age of Globalization*, and *World Class Learners: Educating Creative and Entrepreneurial Students.* He is a recipient of the Early Career Award from the American Educational Research Association and was named one of the 2012 ten most influential people in educational technology by *Tech & Learning Magazine.* He is an elected fellow of the International Academy of Education. His latest book *World Class Learners* has won several awards, including the Society of Professors of Education Book Award (2013) and the Association of Education Publishers Judges' Award and Distinguished Achievement Award in Education Leadership (2013).

 **Homa Sabet Tavangar** is the author of *Growing Up Global: Raising Children to Be At Home in the World* (Random House, 2009), lead author of *The Global Education Toolkit for Elementary Learners* (Corwin, 2014), and contributor to *Mastering Global Literacy*, by Heidi Hayes-Jacobs, ed. (Solution Tree, Nov. 2013). *Growing Up Global* has been hailed by national education and business leaders and media ranging from Dr. Jane Goodall to the BBC, NPR, NBC, ABC, Washington Post.com, Chicago Tribune and Sun-Times, Boston Globe, PBS, Scholastic, Parents Magazine, Rodale, and many more.

Homa's work is sparking initiatives to help audiences from CEOs to kindergartners learn and thrive in a global context—and have fun along the way. She is the series consultant to NBC TV's original production of the animated children's series *Nina's World*, has served as Education Advisor to the Pulitzer Center on Crisis Reporting, and as a Visiting Scholar at the University of Pennsylvania; she is a contributing writer for the *Huffington Post*, PBS, Momsrising, GOOD, Ashoka's Start Empathy, *National Geographic* and Edutopia, among other media, and is a sought-after speaker and trainer around globalization and global citizenship, parenting, globalizing curriculum, empathy, diversity, and inclusion.

Homa spent 20 years working in global competitiveness, organizational, business, and international development with hundreds of businesses, nonprofits, and public organizations before turning her attention to global education. She has lived on three continents, is a Phi Beta Kappa graduate of UCLA and Princeton University's Woodrow Wilson School of Public and International Affairs. She speaks four languages and her religious heritage includes four of the world's major faiths. Passionate around issues of opportunity and equality for women and girls, she has worked on these issues for private companies and the World Bank, and served on various nonprofit Boards, including, currently on the Board and Executive Committee of the Tahirih Justice Center, a national leader protecting immigrant women and girls fleeing violence. She is married and the mother of three daughters.

Emily McCarren is the High School Principal at the Punahou School in Honolulu, Hawaii, the largest single-campus K–12 independent school in the United States. Emily is originally from Vermont. She graduated from Colby College in Maine, where she majored in Spanish and biology and was a two-sport athlete, captaining the alpine ski team and lacrosse team. She holds two master's degrees: one in Spanish literature from the Saint Louis University's Madrid campus and one in educational leadership from the Klingenstein Center at Teachers College, Columbia University. She is completing her PhD in educational technology at the University of Hawaii, where her dissertation examines the role of teacher care on a student's online learning experience. McCarren began her career teaching Spanish and geometry at Swiss Semester, a program for American students in the Swiss Alps. Next, she worked at The Thacher School in Ojai, California, where she taught, coached, and served as a residential advisor for 6 years before joining the faculty at the Punahou School in Honolulu, Hawaii, in 2006. At Punahou, she has taught all levels of Academy Spanish and a year of biology, and she has served as a department head of both Asian-Pacific and European languages and as Academy Summer School director. McCarren was appointed to lead Punahou's Wo International Center in 2012, where she worked to broaden the global perspective of students and faculty while strengthening Punahou's role as a global educational leader.

Gabriel Rshaid is the Headmaster of St. Andrew's Scots School in Buenos Aires, Argentina, the oldest bilingual school in the world, and he is a Professional Development Associate with the Leadership and Learning Center in Denver, Colorado. Gabriel is a former board member of ASCD. He is the author of *Learning for the Future: Rethinking Schools for the 21st Century, The 21st Century Classroom*, and *From Out of This World: Leadership and Life Lessons From the Space Program*. He has presented all over the world on the future of learning and 21st century education, and he has conducted numerous workshops, retreats, and seminars for educators and administrators.

Kay Tucker's vision and passion is to actively engage in defining and creating a culture for world class learning. She collaborates with educators to create ecosystems for sustainable learning, including space, context, and technologies; designs and implements professional development opportunities; and originates systems and tools to impact change. As the World Class Education Specialist at Lone Tree Elementary in Douglas County, Colorado, she is in charge of creating a model of teaching and learning driven by current global educational reform and a world class education based on the thinking of Dr. Yong Zhao. In this model, students learn in an integrated manner as they align their strengths and passions in solving problems within a real-world context. In flexible environments, students navigate curriculum through inquiry and create their own learning pathways while teachers facilitate opportunities, provide resources, and target teach on an as-needed basis. Kay's career in education spans 20 years. She has an undergraduate degree in fine arts from the University of Colorado Boulder and a master's degree in curriculum and instruction from the University of Colorado at Denver.

Introduction

Making World Class Learners

by Yong Zhao

No More Boomerang Kids

"One in five people in their 20s and early 30s is currently living with his or her parents," writes Adam Davidson in a 2014 *New York Times Magazine* article. "And 60 percent of all young adults receive financial support from them. That's a significant increase from a generation ago, when only one in 10 young adults moved back home and few received financial support," Davidson states. The article, "It's Official: The Boomerang Kids Won't Leave," once again brought much attention to the issue of the economic conditions of today's youth, the boomerang generation. For many reasons, mostly the lack of financial resources to be independent, an increasing number of today's youth return to live with their parents, after briefly living away, mostly for pursuing higher education.

Gavin Newton-Tanzer

There are of course exceptions. Gavin Newton-Tanzer is one of them. Not only is he not returning to live with his parents, but he has been helping others to find hope and a future in distant lands. Gavin, a 25-year-old American living in China, has founded several companies and nonprofit organizations

1

that help future youth become financially independent and socially responsible individuals in the globalized world. In 2010, while he was still a student at Columbia University, Gavin founded China Pathway, a company that provides consulting services for Chinese students intending to study abroad and Chinese educational institutions to develop study abroad pathway programs. In 2011, Gavin founded UExcel International Academy, with Compass Education Group, to bring international school programs to public schools in China. Both businesses have been profitable. He has dabbled in other businesses as well, including founding a company for data mining and even a company in movie production. "Neither of which went anywhere, but stemmed from what I saw as opportunities," said Gavin.

Gavin left home upon graduating from Newtown High School in 2007, at the age of 18. He spent a year in China, learning the language and culture, making friends, and honing his organizational skills by serving at the youth volunteer programs in the 2008 Beijing Olympic Games. He now speaks fluent Mandarin Chinese, with a Beijing accent, in addition to French and Spanish. More importantly, Gavin spotted the need for better understanding about China. When he returned to attend college at Columbia University, he started the Global China Connection (GCC) student organization, which now boasts more than sixty chapters in over ten countries. GCC connects thousands of future youth leaders who have a desire and are willing to have a better understanding of China and opportunities in China.

But most impressive is Gavin's new venture, which is transforming education in China. In 2012, he founded Sunrise International Education, a company that develops and provides extracurricular programs in China and ultimately globally. The premier program of Sunrise is the introduction of American-style high school debate in China. After only 2 years, Sunrise programs have trained nearly 100,000 Chinese students and organized tournaments with over 6,000 participants. "We are set to have around 12,000 in tournament[s] this year [2014]," according to Gavin. And Sunrise is working to add two more leagues: drama and business. In many ways, Gavin's programs are having more impact on Chinese students than many government reform efforts, in terms of helping students develop critical thinking skills, communication and public speaking skills, and independent thinking skills, in addition to broadening their educational experiences. By the way, Gavin's company has over twenty employees, and he is expecting to double that number soon.

THE ENTREPRENEURIAL MINDSET

What makes Gavin different from the boomerang kids? The mindset. Gavin has an entrepreneurial mindset that makes him a creator of opportunities and jobs for himself and others. The boomerang kids have the employee mindset that makes them look for jobs that no longer exist. Technology and globalization have transformed our society. Machines and off-shoring have led to the disappearance of traditional middle class jobs—jobs our education has been making our children ready for.

Since there are more boomerang kids than there are graduates like Gavin, it seems reasonable to say that Gavin is an accident, whereas the boomerang kids are the norm. In other words, the boomerang kids are the inevitable, while Gavin is a nice serendipity. This is because our traditional education, by design, produces employees rather than entrepreneurs. The challenge for educators today, if we wish to have fewer boomerang kids, is to figure out how to redesign our education to prepare entrepreneurs like Gavin so they do not happen by accident.

THE IDEAL SCHOOL

That is the purpose of my book *World Class Learners: Educating Creative and Entrepreneurial Students*, which outlines a new design that would turn the Gavin accident into institutional arrangement. The design includes three elements:

1. **Personalization:** Changing education from imposing on students the same standardized content to enabling students to pursue their passions and strengths through student voice and choice, a broad and flexible curriculum, and mentoring and advising.

2. **Product-oriented learning:** Changing pedagogy from just-in-case knowledge transmitting to just-in-time supporting of students' engagement in entrepreneurial activities aiming to produce authentic products and services.

3. **Globalized campus:** Expanding the educational setting from local, isolated, physical spaces to global and virtual spaces to help students develop global perspectives and global competencies.

These three elements form the basic framework of schooling aimed to cultivate globally competent, creative, and entrepreneurial talents needed today. They are about redesigning the three primary aspects of schooling: curriculum, pedagogy, and context (see Figure 1). The ideal school should provide opportunities and resources to enable students to personalize their educational experiences instead of receiving a uniform standardized, externally prescribed, education diet. That is, rather than imposing the same knowledge and skills on all students and expecting them to master the material at the same pace, the school co-constructs a curriculum that follows the students' passions and enhances their strengths. In terms of pedagogy, teachers in the ideal school facilitate student development by supporting and guiding students through an authentic process of creating works that matter to others. To make this possible, the ideal school brings in global resources and engages students in activities that enable students to learn for and with students from all over the world. Simply put, the ideal school is no longer a physical campus.

Figure 1   Elements of Entrepreneur-Oriented Education

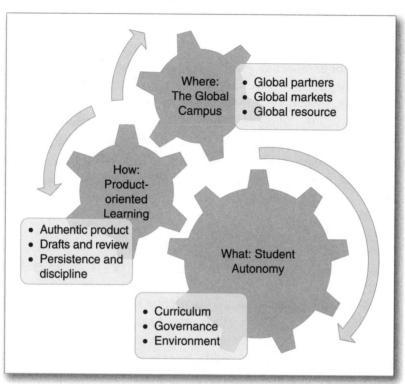

Although the ideal school in the future has all three elements implemented, each element can be implemented separately. A school or teacher can choose to start working on one of the elements and expand to the other two. The elements can also be implemented at different levels depending on the context. An education system at the district, state, or national level can work at the system level to deliver any or all of the three elements. However, a school can do this as well, with the understanding that it can be limited by system-level constraints such as a state or national mandated curriculum. Even individual teachers can implement the redesigned education in their classrooms, again with the understanding that they are constrained by system- and school-level factors such as teacher evaluation, mandated curriculum and assessment, as well as availability of resources.

Limited freedom to make changes in a school or classroom is not desirable, but it is better than maintaining the traditional paradigm. The ultimate goal is a complete transformation of schooling from employee-minded education to entrepreneur-minded education. However, the realities of education today only allow for a gradual evolutionary approach to realizing this transformation. The fact that we cannot have the ideal version of the future right away should not stop us from acting on pieces of it. We can take baby steps before we leap to the future. Thus, all individuals who are involved in education (policy makers, system-level leaders, school principals, and teachers) have a role in making changes, and they also have the capacity and resources to do so.

MAKING THE PARADIGM SHIFT: BOOKS 1, 2, AND 3

World Class Learners presents evidence for why we need the paradigm shift. It also outlines the basic components of the new paradigm as well as areas in which we can begin the work. Since the publication of *World Class Learners* in 2012, there has been growing demand for more practice-oriented guidance and support to help schools and teachers take on the task of transforming the outdated education paradigm. In response, we decided to work on three books, each addressing one of the elements of the new paradigm.

The three books are intended to be practical. In other words, *World Class Learners* is about the *why* and *what* of the educational paradigm shift, and these three books are about the *how* and *what happens*. They are co-written by researchers and practitioners. These books include specific strategies, practical advice, and stories of success and struggle. The strategies, advice, and stories were collected from classrooms and schools that have embarked on the transformation journey. They reflect both promises and challenges of the new paradigm when implemented in current educational settings. Although these books are intended to guide and inspire, they are not meant to be prescriptive, because each school and classroom has its own unique opportunities and constraints.

The organization of the three books is similar. Each book starts with a discussion of theories and definitions of each element, followed by specific suggestions for how each element can be implemented and a description of potential challenges that may work against the implementation. The suggestions are specific to system leaders, school leaders, and classroom teachers. They are also made with the consideration of different realities—thinking (beginning), implementing (intermediate), and expanding (advanced).

Each of the three books addresses one element of the new paradigm. *Personalization and Student Autonomy* provides guidance and suggestions for actions that systems, schools, and classrooms can take to create more autonomy for students and enable them to personalize their educational experiences, to enhance their strengths, and to follow their passions. *Product-Oriented Learning* provides guidance and suggestions for systems, schools, and classrooms to design and develop infrastructures and resources to enable students to engage in authentic projects. *Globalized Campus* aims to help schools and teachers develop global engagement activities for students.

REFERENCES

Davidson, A. (2014, June 20). It's official: The boomerang kids won't leave. *New York Times*. Retrieved July 2, 2015, from http://www .nytimes.com/2014/06/22/magazine/its-official-the-boomer ang-kids-wont-leave.html?_r=0

1

Personalization and Autonomy

by Yong Zhao

Personalization and student autonomy is one of the three elements of a world-class learning paradigm that is necessary for cultivating creative and entrepreneurial students. The other two elements are product-oriented learning and a globalized campus. Personalization and student autonomy is about the *what* of student learning, and this element aims to guide the substance of student educational experiences. Instead of imposing on students the content prescribed by curriculum authorities, we suggest that the educational experience evolve around students' strengths, interests, and passions.

OUTCOME VERSUS PROCESS: DIFFERENT INCARNATIONS OF PERSONALIZATION

To personalize is to design or produce something to meet individual requirements. In education, personalization is often used in the forms of "personalized learning," "personalized education," or "personalized instruction." The term *personalization* is often used interchangeably with *individualization*, and sometimes with *customization*. The general idea is to enable individual students to have an educational experience that meets their individual needs.

Although it has long been recognized that individual students have different needs and high-quality education cannot be "one size fits all," personalization in education has different meanings and realizations in practice because education has many components that can be personalized, individualized, or customized. For example, personalization can happen with the pace of learning by allowing students to learn at their own speed. Personalization can also be employed to enable students to choose when and where they learn. It can also be used in ways that allow students to have a choice of work assignments in the classroom. Furthermore, personalization is a strategy that enables students to demonstrate their learning by creating a product of their own choosing.

Generally speaking, personalization can be put into two categories: process personalization and outcome personalization. Process personalization enables students to enjoy choice in the learning process, whereas outcome personalization allows students to define the end results of their learning. Process personalization is by far the most prominent version in education today because the current education paradigm has a predetermined outcome for all students. That is, no matter how one gets there, we want everyone to get to the same place: mastery of the knowledge and skills prescribed in the authoritative curriculum or standards.

PERSONALIZATION OF THE LEARNING PROCESS

Although the outcome remains the same, the journey to the destination can be personalized to accommodate different needs, abilities, learning styles, and interests of students. Some of the most common aspects of individualization or personalization that have taken place (or should take place) include pace, content, product, learning environments, and assessment.

Personalization of pace: For all sorts of reasons, students come to school with different abilities and thus will acquire the same content at different speeds. To accommodate different abilities in students, schools have been encouraged to allow students to progress at their individual pace. One of the earliest experiments for self-paced learning is programmed instruction advocated by behaviorist psychologists such as B. F. Skinner in the 1960s (Skinner, 1968). Skinner and like-minded individuals relied on technology to enable students to pace their own learning and receive feedback. With the advent of modern computer technologies, individualization of learning pace became more prominent with computer-based learning. Today, the tradition continues in the form of personalized learning with the support of Big Data and learning analytics technology. Personalization of pace can also happen in the classroom by permitting students to work at their own speed. At the school level, one form of personalization is ability grouping or tracking, which puts students into different classes that move at different paces.

Personalization of content: Content can also be personalized to meet individual needs. Although all students in the traditional educational paradigm need to master the same content as prescribed by curriculum standards, they can be exposed to different content that best suits them. For example, following the principles of *differentiated instruction* (Tomlinson, 2001), students can be given different tasks based on their level of understanding of the content to be covered using Bloom's Taxonomy. To accommodate different interests and learning styles, students can also choose different genres of content. For instance, different kinds of texts, novels, or short stories can be used to meet the needs of individual students at different reading levels. The media used to present the content can also be individualized. Some may prefer reading, others listening. Some may learn best from audio, others visual, and still others physical manipulation.

Personalization of product: Students often need to produce some sort of product (e.g., papers, exhibits, or exams) to demonstrate their mastery of the intended content. To accommodate different levels and styles of learning, the type of products expected of students can be personalized. Some students may prefer to write a paper, others may choose to compose a song. Some may demonstrate their learning by constructing a product such as a poster, others may create a multimedia interactive book. Some students may choose to take a traditional test, while others may design a video game.

Personalization of the learning environment: Where and how learning occurs can also be individualized. Although the same standard and content is expected of all students in the traditional paradigm, students may choose to learn in different places, from different sources, and with different arrangements. With the wide accessibility to online resources, students do not need to learn the content from the classroom alone nor do they need to learn from the teacher only. They could also learn from field trips and extended trips. Moreover, students could choose to take courses online from other institutions. In terms of how students can learn, they could learn by themselves, or in collaboration with others. In the classroom, a teacher can create different learning environments to support personalized learning. Teachers may use different grouping strategies to accommodate student working styles and preferences or they can create different physical arrangements in the classroom for different learning purposes.

PERSONALIZATION OF OUTCOME

Personalization of the learning process has tremendous value in improving student learning. It is undoubtedly a major improvement over the traditional one-size-fits-all teaching practices. Thus, personalization has been advocated for decades as an effective approach in the traditional education paradigm to meet the needs of individual students, especially students who have disabilities or are judged to be less ready for certain school tasks. However, it is not enough for cultivating the creative and entrepreneurial talents we need in the new world, as discussed in *World Class Learners: Educating Creative and Entrepreneurial Students* (Zhao, 2012). A different level of personalization is needed: personalization of learning outcomes.

Personalization of learning outcomes takes personalization to a different level by allowing students to pursue their strengths and interests. It does not accept a prescribed curriculum or set of standards as common to all students, as in the traditional paradigm. Thus, the goal of education is not to fix students' deficits measured by external standards. Rather, this level of personalization assumes that all talents, skills, and knowledge are of equal value and thus all learning outcomes are valuable. As a result, instead of forcing or luring all students to master the same knowledge and skills, this approach asks for personalized educational experiences that support the development of individual talent. Recent developments in technology also enable students to have access to global educational resources, hence providing opportunities for students to construct a learning environment that meets their diverse needs.

Strength-based personalization: Allowing students to personalize their outcomes is to enhance their strengths. Thus, strength-based personalization requires teachers to not focus on what the students cannot do. Instead, the teacher looks hard at what each student can do and uses that as a starting point to build an individualized pathway for the student. In other words, rather than having students follow a predetermined curriculum, schools follow students and work with them to co-create the curriculum, which is highly individualized. The curriculum emerges as student learning progresses. To do so, schools need to offer a broad range of courses or other learning activities for students to explore their strengths. In this model, the school becomes a museum of learning opportunities. Students can choose to take advantage of any of these opportunities, as museum visitors would any of the exhibits. Teachers become curators of learning opportunities and also "tour guides" for students. They do not impose but can certainly mentor, motivate, and challenge.

Passion-driven personalization: Personalization can also be driven by students' passions, which can be different from their strengths. That is, what a student may be good at can be different than what he or she is passionate about. Students' interests should be considered as legitimate sources of motivation; what students are passionate about has intrinsic value, although it may or may not coincide with the prescribed curriculum. To support personalization driven by students' interests and passions, schools need to develop mechanisms to identify students' interests. Schools must treat these interests seriously once they are identified, and schools must develop courses and learning activities accordingly.

In summary, personalization of learning outcomes is not mutually exclusive with personalization of process. In fact, it requires all of the different strategies of process personalization. But it goes beyond process personalization by extending personalization beyond a predefined curriculum. Curriculum standards may still be valuable as a guide for specific subjects and domains, should students choose to master that subject or domain. However, students are not forced to learn what has been prescribed, particularly at a prescribed time, location, and pace.

EMPLOYEE-MINDED LEARNING VERSUS ENTREPRENEUR-MINDED LEARNING: AUTONOMY

In the new paradigm of education, students not only engage in personalized education, but they also are given the autonomy to manage their own learning. This is a radical departure from traditional education, in which student learning is managed by adults. In this new paradigm, ownership of learning is transferred to students. Students are responsible for their own learning. If we consider learning as an enterprise, the new paradigm asks that students become entrepreneurs rather than employees.

Students as Employees

In the traditional paradigm of education, students are typically treated as employees—not today's new kind of creative, entrepreneurial employees, but traditional workers on a factory assembly line. Their job is predetermined by authoritative curricula and standards, which include what others have decided to be of value. What is not included is of peripheral importance, if any. Schools and teachers serve as factory managers, who parse the big jobs into smaller ones in the forms of grade-level content, semester courses, weekly units, and even segments of daily lessons. Like factory workers, students clock in at predetermined times each and every day, go to their positions at specified times, work on minute tasks assigned by teachers, and then demonstrate to teachers that they have done their work through quizzes and other forms of assessment. Those who completed the tasks better get better pay (i.e., better grades) than others.

As employees, students have little autonomy in either the outcome or process of learning. The outcome is predetermined. All students are subject to the same expectations. Their interests and individual diversities have next to no bearing on what they are asked to learn. What is supposed to be learned may or may not have any relevance to students' lives or passions. The process is also carefully prescribed. When, where, how, and how fast students learn is dictated with little input from the learner. As a result, all students do what good employees do: Follow orders.

Since students have no autonomy in deciding what, when, where, how, and how fast they learn, they cannot take ownership of their learning, which means they take no responsibility for their learning. In the traditional paradigm, adults (parents, teachers, school leaders, assessment makers, and curriculum developers) take the responsibility for student learning. Consequently, adults are more actively engaged in student learning than are the students themselves. Adults design and develop all sorts of strategies and tricks to motivate students, when, in fact, learning should be self-motivating. Adults devise all sorts of mechanisms to supervise and monitor student learning, when, in fact, students should be managing their own learning. Adults also control all learning resources and opportunities, as well as student time and energy. Most importantly, adults control the power to evaluate students, to label them as competent or incompetent, and to judge whether their learning is legitimate or illegitimate.

In the traditional paradigm, even progressive educational approaches suffer from the factory-based employee mindset. For example, while personalization is a highly valued and pursued approach to improving student learning, quite often the personalization is done to the students. In other words, the personalization is designed and developed by teachers and other adults instead of by the students themselves.

Students as Entrepreneurs

By contrast, we could conceive of students as entrepreneurs. Just like entrepreneurs, who have ownership of their own enterprises and take responsibility for the well-being of those enterprises, students can and should be the owners of their learning enterprises. This shift in paradigm is needed for two reasons. First, students need to learn to be responsible for their own learning enterprises. Second, students are more motivated and more engaged when they take ownership of their learning. When students are more motivated and engaged, they apply more effort and discipline to their work. As a result, they learn better and have less need to be disciplined.

The key to turning students from employee-minded learners to entrepreneur-minded learners is to grant student autonomy. In fact, the word *grant* is misused because all human beings are born autonomous learners. They are born with natural curiosity and an instinctual desire to learn, which is necessary for survival. All individuals want to learn and have the capacity to learn. What they need is an environment rich with stimuli and resources, through which they construct meanings, experiment with hypotheses, and develop skills.

However, in the traditional model of schooling, students are deprived of autonomy and a learning experience prescribed by adults is imposed on them instead. Hence, we need to "grant" autonomy back to students.

Student autonomy means letting students take ownership of their learning, outcomes, and processes. Students are enabled to determine what they would like to learn and to pursue that learning autonomously. However, learning cannot take place in a vacuum. Students need a learning environment that is physically, cognitively, and socially rich. Students also need psychological and emotional support as well as proper moral guidance. It is thus the role of the adults to provide such an environment, support, and guidance.

It is important to recognize that autonomy does not simply mean allowing students to choose from a number of preset pathways or content subjects. Students should have a role in constructing their own pathways. Thus, students should be fully engaged in constructing the learning environment as well. As discussed in *World Class Learners*, students should have full membership in the school community. They co-construct the courses, physical facilities, and social rules for the school. They actively participate in shaping the cognitive capital of the school through participation in selecting and evaluating library and technology resources as well as the staff. Furthermore, they are given voices in school policies and curriculum offerings.

SUMMARY

In order to cultivate creative and entrepreneurial talents, we need to shift to a new education paradigm. The new paradigm is no longer about imposing prescribed content and knowledge on all students. It is about enabling students to have personalized educational experiences determined by them. It is "education of the students, by the students, and for the students." In this paradigm, students are owners of their learning enterprises, instead of employees working to satisfy external standards. Students are driven by passions and interests. These learning enterprises are about enhancing students' strengths, not fixing their deficits. Personalization and autonomy are the hallmarks of the new paradigm.

The new paradigm is predicated on the following beliefs that have been borne out by the research:

- Children are born curious and creative; thus, they have the natural desire to learn. Moreover, children want to do good and are eager to participate in society.
- Children are born different and their home and cultural background further enlarges their differences. Thus, when they come to school, children have different strengths and weaknesses.
- In the postindustrial society, every talent can be of great value when fully developed.
- A prosperous modern society needs a diversity of talents; thus, we need to cherish differences, rather than homogenize them.
- Hence, all children should be provided with a rich environment that enables autonomous and personalized learning.

CHALLENGES

Paradigm shifts do not happen very often and are disruptive in nature. Moving away from the traditional paradigm of requiring all students to learn the same content at the same pace in the same setting will not be easy. It presents tremendous challenges to all aspects of schooling with which we are familiar. Some of the challenges are philosophical. For example, should all students have some common educational experiences? Should they have the same foundational skills and knowledge? The answer is yes, of course. And there are plenty of ways to do so, as the rest of this book demonstrates.

Some challenges are practical. For example, with the existing curriculum mandated by national or state government, how much freedom do schools really have to enable personalized and autonomous learning? Government mandates do indeed pose serious constraints on what schools can do; however, instead of waiting for government to change, schools can find room to implement limited versions of personalized and autonomous learning. This book includes examples of schools and teachers who have successfully done so.

Other challenges may relate to resources. Schools do not have unlimited budgets to create personalized learning for all students. In addition, no school has the staffing to support all students, should we allow each and every student to pursue his or her own interests and passions. Nonetheless, schools and teachers can find innovative ways to maximize personalization of learning, such as enabling students to offer lessons to each other, bringing community resources to schools, and utilizing online resources. This book provides successful examples and specific strategies.

There are other challenges, and we know that the revolution cannot happen overnight. However, we suggest an evolutionary approach to revolution. This book is intended to help schools and teachers start the revolution, gradually and incrementally.

REFERENCES

Skinner, B. F. (1968). *The technology of teaching*. New York, NY: Prentice Hall.

Tomlinson, C. A. (2001). *How to differentiate instruction in mixed-ability classrooms*. Alexandria, VA: ASCD.

Zhao, Y. (2012). *World class learners: Educating creative and entrepreneurial students*. Thousand Oaks, CA: Corwin.

2

Creating Your Own School

What Student-Driven Curriculum Looks Like

by Gabriel F. Rshaid

Here lies the second problem of the move to prescribe knowledge and skills. If one does not know what careers are there in the future, it is difficult, if not impossible, to prescribe the knowledge and skills that will make today's students ready for them.

(Zhao, World Class Learners, *2012, p. 44)*

THE STUDENT-DRIVEN SCHOOL

A student-driven school is one where students take ownership in their learning, make decisions about their learning progress, and are provided with options that allow them first to discover their interests and passions and second, and more importantly, to follow up on them to the full extent of their capabilities. The student-driven school is first and foremost centered on the learning experience and holds itself accountable for stretching students to meet their maximum potential, as opposed to scoring on normed assessments. Teachers in student-driven schools are focused on students and their learning. They do not stigmatize failure but instead promote an environment of risk taking. Teachers share responsibility for providing students not only with needed skills and content but also with the self-motivation to become lifelong learners. Such a school is a fertile breeding ground for entrepreneurial abilities. Students who grow up amid these stimuli will continually be challenged to think about their learning and explore their passions and abilities, and they will be encouraged to speak up, be creative, and not be stymied by failure or frustration.

Featured School

The Dalton School, New York, New York

The Dalton School in New York City is unusual in that, from its foundation in 1919, student choice has been a core element of education at the school. Visionary educator Helen Parkhurst founded Dalton under the Dalton Plan, a system whereby students from a very early age have significant choice in how their education happens, with an emphasis on students pursuing an education that is personally motivating and meaningful. Even at the elementary school level, children meet regularly with an advisor to determine how to shape their studies. At the middle school and high school levels, students not only chose from a wide range of electives, but they also work with their teachers to agree on assignments, research projects, and how to demonstrate proficiency.

I asked Lisa Stifler, the current dean of academic studies, some questions that educators might raise as objections to an environment in which students define how the learning takes place.

How do you make sure
that students master critical content?

Dalton ensures that students learn some core content through a system
of academic credits that requires, for example, four credits or courses in
English literature.

Does making choices about curricula so early in
life, when students are yet immature, short-change
students' later career opportunities?

Lisa feels that in all her years at the school, she has yet to see a graduate
who has made choices that have been detrimental to his or her future
options. Their problem, if anything, is that students want to do too much,
and they tend to overextend themselves in choosing too many projects
and activities. The school is even thinking of making evening courses
available to satisfy the increasing demand for more electives. When there
aren't teachers for a specific subject, their alliance with the Global Online
Academy ensures that courses can be delivered.

What are the foundations of
a student-centered education?

Lisa finds that the encouragement of student-based learning can take
so many different forms—but it necessitates a school philosophy (like
Parkhurst) of trusting children to be natural learners, thinkers, and teachers. Therefore, if (as in Education on the Dalton Plan) there are multiple
pathways toward achieving a goal (or, in a more limiting way, "success"),
there should never be a static moment in a classroom. That is the genius
of Helen Parkhurst—she knew that if everyone in a classroom could be
encouraged as a true "learner," then the dynamic atmosphere of a learning environment would always exist.

   I also spoke with two Dalton students a few days before the beginning
of their senior year. What immediately came across is their fierce loyalty to
the system. They are absolutely sure that they are much better prepared for
college, because they are constantly managing their own course of studies and are therefore better equipped to make decisions and they possess

(Continued)

(Continued)

a greater sense of awareness than students who have been passively led through schooling. With that same uncanny matureness, these students stress that the most rewarding factor related to having choice is how the co-construction of the curriculum with teachers gives them the opportunity to establish more meaningful and lasting relationships with those adults.

According to the Dalton School (2015), "When given responsibility for [an assignment, a pupil] instinctively seeks the best way of achieving it. Then having decided, he proceeds to act upon that decision... Discussion helps to clarify his ideas and also his plan of procedure.... This is real experience.... It is no longer school—it is life." These prophetic words are not a part of a modern-day manifesto calling out for personalization: They were written by Helen Parkhurst in 1922, and they ring even truer now.

The story of how a student-driven education has become the distinctive trait of school culture at Dalton may be unique in terms of its particular circumstances, but there are many lessons that transcend the story itself and that can be applicable to any school.

The next sections will attempt to break down some of the individual components of a student-driven curriculum. It is important to note that none of the ensuing suggestions attempt to constitute either a one-size-fits-all model or a laundry list on how to create a student-driven curriculum. Rather, these are nonlinear ideas and principles that aim to identify the components of such a school.

Principles for a Student-Driven Curriculum

Schools present a very complex reality. Each school and school system is a story in itself. However, it is possible to identify some principles that constitute the backbone of a student-driven curriculum. In this type of curriculum, students:

- Develop the habit of lifelong learning
- Make choices on what topics to learn
- Assume responsibility for the learning process
- Define and self-evaluate desired outcomes

Students Develop the Habit of Lifelong Learning

School should be the initial testing ground for students to become greater protagonists of their own learning. Any specific strategy that points to a student-based customization of the learning experience will certainly prove to be great training for a future that we may yet not know but will irreversibly involve a high degree of awareness regarding learning. In addition, given the frenetic pace of change, and the transient nature of knowledge, there will be a need to learn, unlearn, and relearn.

Here are a few suggested activities that might prepare students for a lifelong learning process:

- Present students with a video or story about some attractive project or interesting development that has recently happened and, after ascertaining whether they found it interesting, ask them to imagine what they would do if they had seen it on their own. The goal is for them to develop the sense of curiosity that is inherent to a lifelong learning attitude and go straight to the Internet to find out whether the project was completed or not, or what happened to it.
- Similarly, show students the development of an exciting new technology and have students discover how the technology works. For example, realistic holograms (e.g., Tupac's "resurrection" at the Coachella festival; *Note:* viewer discretion is advised) are actually pretty simple technologies that students can understand and explain.
- Ask students to find some of their own learning materials on the Internet and work on analyzing the legitimacy of the source and the author as well as the usefulness of the material. This will prepare them to be discerning agents able to vet content found on the Internet.
- Model what lifelong learning looks like. It cannot be stressed enough that adults must model a lifelong learning mindset, particularly teachers who need to make conscious efforts to share their adult learning experiences with students. Inviting community members to take part in the learning process, either via giving talks on subject-related topics or acting as mentors with

project-based learning, can also reinforce the message that learning is not restricted to the school years.

Students Make Choices on What Topics to Learn

The element of choice has an added benefit when it comes to fostering an entrepreneurial and creative mindset. In terms of the desired skills that characterize world class learners who will be enterprising and able to seize upon a world of opportunity, the discernment process of what needs to be learned is an integral and quintessential part of the process. If we wish for our students to be dynamic problem solvers, we need to nurture their ability to gain knowledge on a need-to-know basis, directly related to creating something or finding a solution to a problem at hand. By training students at an early age to make their own learning decisions, we pave the way for future entrepreneurial thinkers who will be prepared to tackle open-ended questions head-on.

Some examples on how students can make choices are as follows:

- Have class discussions prior to studying a topic. That is, explore the theme of a unit of studies and ask students to identify which topics we would need to know in order to learn the unit. Gradually, students can develop the healthy habit of trying to discern what the learning needs to be.
- Present students with a problem to be solved that exceeds their current grasp of certain skill sets, such as reading a map. Then set up a collective class discussion that attempts to break down how to tackle the problem, what data need to be found, what new skills need to be learned, and so on. Taking this idea one step further, different class groups can learn one skill or subtopic and then present it and teach it to the rest of the class, and students are thereby also engaging in collaborative learning.

Students Assume Responsibility for the Learning Process

When students have a say in and influence over their own learning experiences, they start assuming responsibility for the learning process, which is a habit that will serve them well in being independent creative thinkers in the future.

Examples of student choice in classroom activities are as follows:

- Present students with the goals and learning outcomes for a unit and give them freedom to choose how to achieve those goals. This can be done at any age, from choosing stations in kindergarten to selecting optional topics within a higher-level Advanced Placement course syllabus. The point we are trying to make is that students are capable of taking positive actions to increase their learning and their enjoyment of their learning.
- Allow students to hand in assignments on their own schedule. Expect them to manage the progress of their own work on their own time, with the only deadline being the end of the marking period.
- Present students with a series of tasks that need to be accomplished throughout the unit to demonstrate mastery and have the students themselves decide in what sequence they will complete them.

Students Define and Self-Evaluate Desired Outcomes

Redefine the system of standards and accountability so that the focus is not just on the content to be learned and specific skills to be acquired. Individual educators, or even schools, are not necessarily able to change systemwide educational policies, but there are some practical ways to instigate a gradual shift in the prevailing mindset regarding what constitutes educational success. Reassess expected outcomes to include student ownership of learning, greater awareness about the learning process, and intrinsic motivation to learn to allow students greater engagement in the learning process. This might be accomplished when:

- Students can design their own parallel outcomes in relation to imposed standards and hold themselves accountable for meeting their particular learning goals.

At the beginning of every unit, students write out explicit goals that they will accomplish by the end of the unit. These objectives would be measurable in a way such that students themselves can gauge their attainment throughout the learning process.

- Teachers and administrators can themselves evaluate and report on the development of some of these redefined outcomes by students, sending a powerful message about what really matters at school. Adhering to alternative standards that are more attuned to what the school considers of value can be a way around the perceived gap between what educators in the school deem to be important and standards that are imposed upon them externally.

- School awards can be instituted that reward the skills and achievements identified as valued. These can serve to provide incentives for students to pursue the development of some of the skills associated with creativity, decision making, and initiative. In a student-driven curriculum, students have greater opportunities to exercise their leadership, and the school system should also recognize those students who excel and embody those desired characteristics.

STRATEGIES FOR A STUDENT-DRIVEN CURRICULUM

The strategies below offer some concrete ideas to classroom teachers, administrators, and policy makers who want to take significant steps toward a student-driven curriculum. Acknowledging that every school has its own unique context, these strategies should be implementable in most contexts.

In the Classroom

Encourage Student Choice

An entry-level recommendation for a student-driven curriculum involves providing students with choices within a pre-established curriculum, based on their interests. From a very early age, children can be trained to choose different activities or to explore subtopics within a subject that they can later share with their peers, in order to gain a sense of autonomy.

Examples of specific strategies would involve the following:

- Students choosing from among a menu of topics within a unit, all of which will be different ways to achieve the learning objectives. For example, in a geography lesson, choose from various regions to explore; in history, opt between studying various historic events that all relate to the same objective.
- In terms of activities, students can make options from a very early age and can choose, even in kindergarten, from various corners or activities. Some activities entail having teachers present students with various pathways that include playing with an iPad or tablet, building something, engaging in a play-based simulated game, or drawing up a poster, and then asking which of the stations were more enjoyable, as a way to start generating the reflex of reflecting upon one's own learning and preferences. Further down the road in schooling, students can select from various assignments that may include very different forms (i.e., a written test, a PowerPoint presentation, a video, a poster, etc.) in order to demonstrate that they have mastered the desired skills and content.

Encourage Students to Play an
Active Role in Designing Their Learning

As a teacher, work with students to determine how each individual approaches the learning process, gathers resources, and investigates within an inquiry-based process that adheres to the principles of 21st century learning.

Students can work to:

- Select topics of investigation/research topics
- Find resources (online and otherwise) to contribute to their learning
- Set a schedule and a pace for personalized learning that matches their unique learning style

- Plan together with teachers how best to carry out the learning activities involved. Even if done only occasionally during the length of the school year, designing a whole unit gives students valuable insight into tackling more complex learning challenges.

Monument Mountain Regional High School has developed the Independent Project (a school within a school), featuring a section of this public high school that is entirely run by students, with no adults involved whatsoever. This extreme example of student ownership has students deciding on an inquiry topic every Monday and then assuming responsibility for their own learning by producing a report on their progress that same Friday. Students opt for this study modality for a full semester and are aware that only through their own success will they be able to sustain it in the face of critics who are unsettled by an entirely student-driven project.

Matthew Vernon Whalan (2014), a student at Monument sums it up very well:

> I participated in this project from my sophomore year to my senior year, each year for one semester, and I heard both endless praise and endless criticism. It wasn't whether those of us in the program doubted whether the project would work, or whether we would succeed. We knew we would have to for the project to continue, and for the most part, we did. Students produced amazing work. But we also knew some people—and some students—would be upset by the very existence of the project.

Giving students greater ownership and agency is a step in the right direction. It is doable in any context.

Offer Students Choice in How They Are Evaluated

Allowing students to choose how they demonstrate their acquired knowledge is an integral part of any student-driven curriculum. Self-assessment constitutes an essential skill to be developed, since all individuals in the context of continuous learning must be able to assess whether they have learned or not and if they are ready to move forward. Students can also write assessment instruments and rubrics for the evaluation of their peers.

Collaborate

When developing a student-driven curriculum, there are a multitude of opportunities for students to assume varied roles in the learning process. These include reviewing, critiquing, providing constructive feedback to peers, and performing necessary tasks. One of the distinctive characteristics of entre-preneurs is the ability to function as an effective member of a team, and student choices within the curriculum allow for plentiful opportunities for that to happen.

Assign Product-Oriented Learning Projects

One very important dimension of product-oriented learning is that students be free to frame the problem and design the project. Very often, project-based learning can be quite teacher-centric, in that a teacher comes up with an interesting and attractive project to develop or a problem to be solved, and the teacher is also the ultimate audience for the project. However, engaging students in the decision of what project to tackle and coaching them in developing a protocol to approach it adds the benefit of giving students the opportunity to exercise their creativity and agency and, equally importantly, to ask reflectively what needs there are and what would constitute a meaningful challenge.

Coming up with the questions themselves and satisfying needs is intrinsic to the entrepreneurship process. Allowing students to formulate and solve their own projects, in addition to designing a protocol and related assessment model in terms of their own defined outcomes of success, enables students to develop the skills necessary for them to thrive in future workplace scenarios.

In the School

Allow for Student Choice in Course Selection

Nurture students' unique talents and learning abilities by allowing them to choose their elective subjects. Prevalent thinking stipulates that, especially in advanced and challenging courses, students who are allowed more freedom of choice are more likely to succeed because they will be working on topics that are of personal interest to them.

Provide Instruction Alternatives Outside the School

Often, schools will find that students are requesting instruction in obscure and niche subjects, for which the school has no teacher—and no budget. In these cases, it is advisable to try out one of the numerous massive online open courses or tailor-made courses that provide online instruction, and to have a teacher act as a mentor to or facilitator for the group or individual. Most of these courses include assessment modules, so the school itself can tap into them for formal evaluation and accountability purposes.

The seemingly problematic situation can be transformed into a 21st century model in which teachers play the role of co-learners, since they themselves do not have subject matter expertise in the topic in question. In this scenario, students will be accessing resources online and learning in the same way that adults access knowledge and skills outside of formal learning settings.

Have Students Lead Extracurricular Activities

Extracurricular activities have long been a staple for student choice, since they epitomize all that is good about student choice: students get to select an activity that they enjoy, in a nonacademic setting, with no grades and often with the powerful incentive of competition. The school may not have the resources to offer a very wide range of extracurricular activities, so it would be a powerful idea to have students propose and then run their own.

In every school, there are students who specialize in some hobby or sport outside of school. Providing these individuals with support, guidance, structure, and a protocol for developing these offerings (i.e., scheduling, organization, practices, coaching duties, performances) will not only go a long way in terms of broadening the choice for students, but it will also help them gain very valuable leadership and entrepreneurial skills.

In the School System

Allow for Personalized Graduation Roadmaps

The traditional path to graduation involves fulfilling a set curriculum. A more radical concept of schooling involves having students complete personalized pathways with a substantial element of choice, whereby instead of ticking off subjects and content, they need to demonstrate mastery of certain increasingly complex tasks as they proceed, in a nonsequential way and with a wide variety of assessment methods and instruments.

In such a context, school would serve more as a loosely bound environment in which teachers would act as counselors and advisors, mentoring students in particular tasks or projects. These meaningful tasks should ideally be rooted in real-life problems and should present progressively more difficult sets of challenges.

Develop Districtwide Student-Led Projects

Starting in 2000, the province of Queensland, Australia, developed the Rich Tasks initiative, which applied to all schools in that province. Rich tasks were systematically interspersed throughout the curriculum, and they were a series of transdisciplinary tasks that constitute "a reconceptualization of the notion of outcome as demonstration or display of mastery; that is, students display their understanding, knowledge, and skills through performance on transdisciplinary activities that have an obvious connection to the wide world" (Grauf, 2001).

Similarly, districts can mandate interdisciplinary student projects that are more oriented to the entrepreneurship paradigm, in which students, along the curriculum, will have to make choices and decisions that increasingly reflect real-life situations they may encounter as they age. These projects would form an integral part of the curriculum and would incorporate many of the previously outlined principles.

Institute a Student Council for the District

Similarly to how student body government is very much a part of the everyday landscape of schools, in order to develop a truly student-centered school, districts could institute a districtwide student council with representation from all of the different schools in the district. Members of this council would aim to:

- Explicitly relay student voice to central office leaders and staff;
- Interact with the key decision makers in the district, offering their views and perspectives on schools in general and on curriculum decisions in particular; and
- Act as a general advisory board to the superintendent, scheduling meetings on a regular and systematic basis.

This strategy not only intends to foster an increased level of student participation across the district, but it also helps students from different schools collaborate and establish links as well as learn how to operate in real-life situations regarding policy making and decisions. In addition, this strategy sends a very powerful message for teachers in particular and the community in general regarding the importance of students' choice and voice in the district.

OVERCOMING CHALLENGES

As with any attempt at innovation, the development of a student-driven curriculum has its own unique set of challenges and, when faced with a still largely traditional environment of school systems, giving students choice and voice in drawing up the curriculum is undoubtedly quite countercultural and may meet a fair amount of resistance. The following sections attempt to address some of those voices of doubt, knowing well enough that there are no easy answers to most of these questions. The goal here is to try to bring to light the many positives of giving students a more active role in their learning.

A Student-Driven Curriculum Is Not Rigorous

The revered concept of rigor is the so-called "white elephant in the room" whenever any educational innovation is presented. There is a fear that anything that is enjoyable, open ended, or creative or that promotes "soft" skills leads to lowered standards and decreases the quality of education.

The key to refuting this objection lies in redefining rigor in terms of outcomes that are not solely based on complying with external standards but instead refocus on the principles outlined in this and other chapters in this book. Within the new knowledge paradigm, a rigorous curriculum is one that prepares students for dealing with a world of uncertain outcomes and infinite choices. In addition, a rigorous curriculum develops the habits and motivation for lifelong learning in students. If it is designed conscientiously, a student-driven curriculum can most definitely meet the requirements of rigor.

All Students Should Learn a Given Set of Skills and Material

There is merit in the observation that all students should acquire literacy in language, math, and certain core skills. Thankfully, student choice is not at all incompatible with a solid knowledge base and ensuring that students meet a given set of standards.

A personalized curriculum builds on students' strengths and actually comes up with the best ways for students to learn, including acquiring prescribed content if necessary. Allowing students to make choices and exercise initiative and ownership in their learning is a more efficient way to ensure that learning takes place and is significant, as opposed to educating students such that are drilled to comply with standardized tests and promptly forget what they learned.

Student choice negates the role of the adult.

Ceding some of the decision making to students elevates the role of the adult to a higher order challenge of, in Michelangelo's timeless words, "uncovering the Angel in the stone." The problem is not whether the teacher's authority is put into question when allowing students to make choices, but how teachers can rekindle their vocational call through a renewed mindset, more at the service of students rising up to their full potential.

It's More Work!

True! A student-driven curriculum that allows greater breadth, depth, and flexibility does entail a greater amount of work as well as logistics and scheduling complications, but all for a worthwhile effort.

As the students at the Dalton School affirm, being able to make their own decisions about their schooling may initially be daunting, but they know that it will better prepare them for taking full advantage of the opportunities they will be offered at the college level. Dalton students pointed out an additional benefit of the extra work—student-driven curriculum leads to better, stronger, healthier relationships between teachers and students, since the empowerment of students to take greater agency in their learning levels the field and helps teachers move away from the default mode in which adults are solely responsible for making decisions. At the end of the day, it is those relationships that constitute the most important outcome of any school and remain with students as lifelong impressions of mentorship.

Choice Does Not Work for All Students

Images that come to mind include students who do not express themselves in class discussions, who never volunteer answers to questions, who are reticent in and out of class, and who would probably find it very challenging to take ownership and make their own choices. Once again, the real issue is deeper and it relates to preparing students for a world of infinite choice and opportunity, and that, whether they like it or not, the world of today and tomorrow is not a good place to surrender to other people's decisions.

Bringing in an element of choice even from kindergarten onward will be beneficial to develop decision making skills, while respecting the individual personalities of students and clearly not trying to force them out of who they are. Even if not all students end up being entrepreneurs, we will nonetheless serve them well by positively challenging them to take control of their learning and become more aware of the choices they will have to make in the future.

Existing curriculum and standardized assessments constraints make a student-centered curriculum utopian.

It would be naïve to ignore that the current environment, irrespective of grade level and geographical location, is not very conducive to flexibility and student choice. The shining examples of schools that are prominently featured do enjoy, in most of those cases, a great degree of flexibility and are championed by leaders with enough self-esteem to defy conventional wisdom and the educational establishment.

However, as we hopefully have been able to convey in the previous sections, there are many opportunities for student choice and personalization even within restrictive educational systems. A lot can be achieved in terms of fostering independence and autonomy by allowing students even limited choices within a set curriculum. Think of student-driven curriculum as a mindset that is embodied and transmitted by adults by virtue of their actions, how they conduct themselves, and how students are assessed. Educators with this mindset can find opportunities within existing systems and constraints, rather than wait for a systemic reform.

It Would Be Chaotic

In this respect, it is time to acknowledge that we live in a nonlinear, unfathomable, and intrinsically uncertain world and that regardless of what the future looks like, the messiness will not change. It is fitting then that school mirrors, to the extent feasible, the world to which our students belong. We need to embrace a creative chaos, rather than futilely attempt to resist it.

Reflection

In order to embrace a better and more meaningful model of schooling, it is essential that educators help students find and enjoy their passions. A student-driven curriculum is instrumental to awakening their interests. From their first years of schooling, student-driven curriculum compels students to ask themselves questions, to discern their likes and dislikes, and to identify their talents as well as ways in which those talents can serve society.

Activity #1: A Primer for Independent Learning

Participants

Depending on the nature of the topic, this activity can be done by any group of students. It can also be simulated by teachers in a workshop setting by choosing a topic that is outside of most people's area of knowledge, such as whether there is life on Mars or the principles of operation of an ion engine. The goal is to start from a topic that seems unassailable and prove that lifelong learning can be achieved with self-directed learning.

Objective

The activity targets students acquiring lifelong learning skills by researching and finding information for a given topic in a systematic way that takes into account the validation of the sources, using a progressive approach to narrowing down the scope of the information that needs to be found, and annotating the resources for the collaborative sharing of knowledge.

Process

A learning topic will be presented by the teacher to the class, who, preferably in small groups, will attempt to find resources and related information for the learning of the topic, which can be as complex and as broad as required, depending on the nature of the subject at each student level. The following are examples of possible topics:

Very broad topics: Examples include the water cycle, World War II, weather on Mars, or the Industrial Revolution. For these topics, the goal would be to help students narrow down a very broad topic to the most important elements and be able to discern which are the most relevant subtopics within the theme as well as find related resources.

Specific topics: Examples of specific topics include causes of the Boer War in South Africa, factors that influence viscosity in a liquid, or the life and works of a certain artist. For such topics, conversely, the objective is more to dive deeper—that is, to find detailed and valuable learning materials regarding a narrowly defined topic.

Open-ended or controversial topics: Such topics could be the existence of life on Mars, the uncertainty principle for quantum mechanics, analyzing the causes for inflation in underdeveloped countries, the dual nature of light as a particle and a wave, or anything else that does not have a right or wrong answer but can still be analyzed by learning facts regarding the intended question. These topics lend themselves to objectively analyzing known facts and circumstances, gradually progressing toward an educated best estimate of what the answer would potentially be.

There are, of course, all kinds of other topics that may fall anywhere in between these categories. The protocol for undertaking the research entails the following:

1. Analyze the problem or question and its circumstances based on an initial reading or consultation with easy-to-understand websites, like Wikipedia. This first stage

involves an initial understanding of what the problem is about and how it can be tackled. In the process, students try to determine what the critical factors are and how to refine the search in order to look for what is relevant given the topic, and, consequently, they also become better at gauging how to discern which resources may prove to be valuable.

2. Refine the search query through an iterative process in finding resources that relate to each of the subtopics that pertain more readily to the theme being studied.

3. Validate the sources. This very important step in the process entails verifying the accuracy, credibility, and academic credentials of each of the sources found. Students will be directed toward finding out, for each of the links, who owns the page, who is responsible for that particular site, or if there is an author of the article (to investigate their level of expertise on the topic). Students will also scan the text for unsubstantiated assumptions or pieces of information, or any other step that teachers may consider in discerning whether the source is valid or not. Being able to discern the validity of a source is a fundamental process in the learning experience of students and should be used and extrapolated to all other learning activities.

4. Post an annotated list of links online. The final stage involves students posting their links in a common blog or online resource so that other students can learn from what they have found. Students also provide a brief commentary on what the proposed link or article contains and how it can help the learning of the subject at hand.

It would be a good idea to model this activity with adults, both to understand the intricacies of the process as well as to reflect firsthand on the independent, student-centered learning experience.

Reflection

When done with students as well as with adults in a workshop setting, engaging in a debriefing/reflection session is always an interesting exercise. Debriefing also enhances our awareness about the learning process. Some of the following issues can be addressed:

- What is the new nature of knowledge and how does it lend itself to such a process? The Internet world is no longer a world in which there is one form of knowledge. How does this impact our learning approach?
- What are the risks of such a model? Can students come up with erroneous/inaccurate information?
- How does the independent learning process relate to the entrepreneurial mindset? How can we draw a parallel between researching and finding out a topic, compared with the real-life process of creation and entrepreneurship?
- Are there any other safeguards that need to be built into such a protocol to ensure that the learning is not compromised in the independent environment?

ACTIVITY #2: SETTING LEARNING GOALS

Participants

This activity is appropriate for all students, particularly middle school and high school students.

Objective

During the activity, students will write out at least five learning goals.

Process

Activity 2 allows 45 minutes to brainstorm learning goals and 15 minutes for reflection with the larger group.

1. Define the problem, project, or topic. Carefully define the question to be answered, a project to be developed and created, a problem to be solved, or a topic that needs to be studied. Of these four possibilities, we will focus on a topic that needs to be studied.

2. Determine what needs to be learned and why.

- What are the most important subthemes within the topic?
- Why do we want to learn this?
- What are the applications of this theme or topic?
- Which are the key factors for the understanding and learning for this particular topic?
- What questions should be answered in order to gain proficiency in the learning of the topic?

3. Write learning outcomes. Write out expectations, or learning outcomes, as unit objectives against which you can measure attainment. Learning outcomes should be a focus for students during the topic study so that they remain conscious of what is expected of them throughout the learning unit.

Reflection

Students reflect on how assuming an active role in their learning made them feel. Respond to the following questions:

- Is academic rigor compromised by having students actively participate in the goal-setting process? Why or why not?
- Should the teacher guide the process or just act as a catalyst/facilitator? Why?
- How can a teacher ensure that the outcomes and learning goals are compatible with existing curricula?
- Do you think it would be unsettling for students to have to write their own learning goals? Why or why not? If so, how can teachers help students gain confidence in setting their own learning objectives?

- Did you experience any "aha" moments or realizations while going through this exercise? If so, please share them with the group.

Apply the learning outcomes generated by this activity in future study units to guide students in evaluating their own learning.

ACTIVITY #3: GRADUATION ROADMAPS

Participants

This activity is geared toward adult educators, as a first exercise toward designing graduation roadmaps at their school site.

Objective

Draw up an alternative graduation path that highlights the desired skills and capabilities necessary for the work force of the future. Use this as a parallel checklist alongside your current graduation requirements.

Process

Come up with a clearly defined activity or role (the example below involves being a server at a restaurant). Draft a list of essential skills and accomplishments required of that role. Based on the list of skills and accomplishments, create a path toward graduation that completely prepares students to fill that role.

Steps in Creating a Graduation Roadmap

1. Write out the desired behaviors and expectations of a given profession. For example, a proficient server at a restaurant would be able to:

- Make recommendations from the restaurant menu
- Inform diners about the different ingredients involved in each of the dishes

- Maintain immaculately clean tables
- Take orders from clients and convey orders without errors to the kitchen staff
- Do the same with the cashier in order to ensure that the proper items are billed
- Take fully loaded dishes to and from the kitchen and tables

It is not necessary to outline in excruciating detail all of the tasks that are involved in a given profession; rather, exemplify what learning outcomes are expected from graduates when they finish school.

Sorting Out the "Good to Have" From the Essentials

A subsequent step involves discriminating what is essential—that is, those outcomes that are indispensable regarding what makes a good waiter and which of the other outcomes are desirable but not absolutely necessary, so that some waiters can specialize in certain aspects of the task and complement the strengths of their colleagues on the team. These, in terms of graduation requirements, will distinguish the core requirements (those that every student has to comply with) from the optional ones (those that contribute to the education of students but are not considered mandatory for every student). Thus, you could conceive a graduation roadmap that includes certain mandatory elements and some others in the form of credits that students may opt for in order to complete the requirements.

Training Tasks

The following stage has to do with writing out training tasks, courses, and projects that are related to the learning outcomes and constitute discernible milestones that prospective waiters, in this case, have to meet. In our example, these could be the following:

- Over an extended period of time, carry orders to the kitchen with a certain predefined percentage of discrepancy as a tolerance margin for errors
- Pass a test regarding information from the menu
- Receive consistent good reviews from customers during the training
- Accomplish a series of predefined physical tasks regarding the carrying of dishes to and from the kitchen

The whole idea, of course, is not to engage in a mathematical exercise, but rather to illustrate the point that graduating from school may not necessarily just entail passing a series of tests in concatenated cumulative subjects. It may be argued that the example at stake is related to a task-oriented role and, as such, it is easier to narrow down and define than general education objectives; however, this example nonetheless, serves to exemplify the entire thought process, which, obviously, would be far more complicated in terms of defining the outcome of a school.

The final phase is related to determining, as previously suggested, a protocol that requires successful graduates to complete a certain number of these tasks in nonsequential order and defining which of the tasks are absolutely decisive in terms of the educational outcomes and which of them can be optional, thus defining a personalized roadmap for every student.

Within the set example (which focuses deliberately on a simple task as an easy example), a graduation roadmap for the aspiring waiter would look like the following:

- Can demonstrate, via a set of ad hoc evaluations, the ability to memorize and recall orders from a certain number of customers and then serve them their choice
- Complies with evaluations of the individual's knowledge of the dishes on the menu, nutritional information, alternatives, and other related information
- Designs a full restaurant menu, as a way to demonstrate the individual's knowledge about food and cooking

- Provides a panel of experts with successful and well-balanced recommendations for a meal based on the theoretical customer's profiles
- Successfully handles simulated crisis situations and provides timely and adequate service responses to customer requests under ad hoc situations that stray from normal restaurant situations, such as special dietary requests, cases in which dishes that are not available and other recommendations must be provided, and so forth
- Has a consistent record regarding personal appearance and presentation as specified in the restaurant norms and rules and procedures
- Successfully passes the dishes-handling tests, which involve going to and from the kitchen and performing a set physical-related tasks in an allotted period of time
- Works ten lunch shifts and ten dinner shifts at the restaurant with a positive review rate from customers (*Note:* this would be a final task)

Reflection

The goal is to use this example as a catalyst to spur a discussion on how an educational graduation roadmap would look. During a brainstorming session after the activity, the following questions can be targeted:

- Should certain tasks be correlative (i.e., one cannot be started until a previous requirement is completed)?
- Should there be a summative end-of-school graduation project?
- Would a nonsequential series of tasks conspire against the structuring of school schedules and render them almost impossible?
- It is implicit in such a model that age grouping is no longer the driving factor in school scheduling and class assignment. How do we feel about mixed age groupings?
- Are rigor and high standards compromised in such an approach?

REFERENCES

Dalton School. (2015). Overview. Retrieved from http://www.dalton .org/philosophy/dalton_plan

Grauf, E. (2001). New basics: Queensland trials a curriculum for tomorrow. Retrieved July 5, 2015, from http://www.acsa.edu .au/pages/images/2001_new_basics_qld_trials_a_curriculum .rtf.doc

Vernon Whalan, M. (2014, July 14). Monument Mountain's "Independent Project": Risk and opportunity. Retrieved from http://theberkshireedge.com/monument-mountains-indepen dent-project-risk-opportunity/

Zhao, Y. (2012). *World class learners: Educating creative and entrepreneurial students.* Thousand Oaks, CA: Corwin.

RESOURCES

Bogdan, P. (2011, February 18). Student-centered learning strategies for math and other subjects. Retrieved from http://www.edutopia .org/blog/student-centered-learning-activities-paul-bogdan.
Bogdan is a former traditional teacher who reinvented himself to be "reborn as a student-centered teacher" and provides a series of strategies for mathematics and other subjects.

Coalition of Essential Schools. (2015). Benchmarks. Retrieved from http://essentialschools.org/benchmarks/10/
This website provides benchmarks for student-centered teaching and learning, as well as a list of descriptors of observable student behaviors with a learner-centered paradigm.

Hopkins, G. (2003, March 28). Revive reviews with student-created study guides. Retrieved from http://www.educationworld .com/a_lesson/03/lp306-04.shtml
This website provides a series of detailed lesson plans on how students can create a study guide for their peers.

Iowa CORE. Characteristics of effective instruction: Student-centered classrooms. Retrieved from http://www.iglls.org/files/class room_brief.pdf
This paper describes how student-centered classrooms can constitute effective instruction.

Powell, M. (2013, December 24). 5 ways to make your classroom student-centered. Retrieved from http://www.edweek.org/tm/articles/2013/12/24/ctq_powell_strengths.html

Powell, a math and science teacher, offers practical advice on how to effectively make the classroom student-centered.

Reiken, C. (2014, April 21). Why I changed to a choice-based art curriculum. Retrieved from http://www.theartofed.com/2014/04/21/why-i-changed-to-a-choice-based-art-curriculum/

This article provides reflections from two art teachers who incorporated choice as a defining element in their art courses.

Vernon Whalan, M. (2014, July 14). Monument Mountain's "Independent Project": Risk and opportunity. Retrieved from http://theberkshireedge.com/monument-mountains-independent-project-risk-opportunity/

This website is a personal testimonial from one of the students in the school on how the Independent Project program can impact young people's lives.

3

Helping Students Turn Strengths Into Passions

by Homa Tavangar

What lies behind us and what lies before us are tiny matters compared to what lies within us.

—*Henry S. Haskins*

Creative entrepreneurs are passionate individuals who capitalize on their strengths rather than spending time making up for their weaknesses.

(Zhao, World Class Learners, *2012, p. 175)*

Featured School

Carrboro High School, Carrboro, North Carolina

Social studies teacher, Matt Cone, has learned a great deal about culti-vating passionate, globally conscious learners in his 13 years of teaching. As he related to us, he thought that if he conveyed the gravity of issues that he personally cared about (such as the AIDS epidemic or the war in the Congo), his students would also find causes and topics that they were passionate about. In fact, he found the opposite to be true.

As Matt adjusted his approach to teaching, always with an eye on cultivating students' strengths and turning these into passions, he and his students began to realize some remarkable successes. Students—many of whom had never taken an honors class and came from families in which no one had previously attended college—mastered complex aca-demic subjects usually reserved for university seminars; built relation-ships with global leaders like health pioneer Dr. Paul Farmer and World Bank President Dr. Jim Kim; raised over $125,000 for nonprofit organiza-tions serving Haiti; and presented at conferences that had never before heard from high school students.

These milestones tell a bigger story. Students gained a new-found level of academic confidence by drawing on their latent strengths, were shown respect by being given the freedom to investigate various top-ics that interested them (within a larger theme), became motivated to learn the material more thoroughly than just about any other subject matter they had encountered, and were not deterred by setbacks or "failures." This convergence, at the intersection of pursuing personal interests while building on individual strengths, helped students to discover and begin developing their passions. In "10 Tips for Discover-ing Your Child's Strengths," Jenifer Fox (2009) explains that "strengths are different than interests because strengths are innate and children will be drawn to them for their entire lives, while interests may be fleeting. When strengths and interests combine, children can develop passions. Strengths can be developed at a very early age and parents/teachers can help out."

> This convergence, at the intersection of pursuing personal interests while building on individual strengths, helped students to discover and begin developing their passions.

PRINCIPLES FOR CULTIVATING YOUR PASSIONS

Although the steps that Matt Cone took to spur this process weren't complicated, it took years of trial and error to get there (M. Cone, personal communication, August 4, 2014). The lessons learned reflect key principles we've seen across other innovative learning environments. They are particularly relevant to illuminating how to develop personalization in learning, because they reflect the shift in moving from imposing standardized content to offering students voice and choice, which invariably helps students realize their passions and build the agility to respond to changing interests, market conditions, and opportunities—stepping out of an "employee mindset."

Become Teachers and Students Who Empathize

- At the heart of each step is the principle of *empathy*. Teachers should try to put themselves in their students' shoes as the students experience the process of discovering new concepts and tapping their own strengths. Students in turn should practice empathy as they consider real needs in the world, allowing these needs to touch them personally so that they will stand up for something, not simply stand by.

Discern What You Are Passionate About

- Entrepreneurial efforts begin with passions. As has been documented over and over again in business cases, successful entrepreneurial ventures usually begin as an outgrowth of two factors working together: channeling a passion *and* filling a need in the market. Even if the passion is not apparent at the outset, understanding this principle can help students begin a learning quest that starts with questions not answers. On the flip side, a student's passions could serve as the starting point, and teachers and students can plan backward from there for learning and lessons that can build an entrepreneurial experience.

Connect Your Passion With Your Entrepreneurial Venture

- Draw clear connections between passions and entrepreneurial ventures or career possibilities. An example later in this chapter shares how one of Matt Cone's students became a prominent health professional, spurred by the passion-nurturing strategies in Cone's class. A medical school track might not traditionally be considered an entrepreneurial path, but a healthy dose of exposure to innovators, nonjudgmental brainstorming on (traditional or nontraditional) career possibilities with an entrepreneurial component, and other environmental factors can expose students to thinking entrepreneurially for any career they might choose.

Listen Actively

- Practice active, purposeful listening. As Rory Newcomb, who leads technology integration at the American School in Bombay, a school dedicated to innovation, put it: "My role in the classroom is not to deliver content. It's all about listening—and listening some more. You listen to find out, what do students wonder about? What are their frustrations, their passions? My job is to listen and then make connections, to turn them into knowledgeable networkers as opposed to knowledgeable workers." (Boss, 2013).

Cultivate Your Passions

- Cultivate your own passions. As the adult leader in the class or group, sharing your own experience in cultivating and channeling your passions will serve as a powerful example (although it won't be enough to spur a diverse group's interests, as Matt Cone discovered). If you haven't identified your own passions in or outside the classroom, take the strategies discussed throughout this chapter to find your passions. If you feel ready, share your own journey with your students so they realize a life-long learning approach and see you learning, trying, (possibly) failing, reflecting, and repeating.

Share Your Passion With Others

- Don't feel alone in your efforts. Whether you have support from family and friends, colleagues in your building, or a virtual professional learning network on Twitter that might gather once at a professional conference, learning and sharing can help you articulate not just the passions you are developing in your profession but also the ways you introduce new innovations in your classroom.

STRATEGIES FOR FOSTERING PASSION-BASED LEARNING IN YOUR CLASS, SCHOOL, OR DISTRICT

1. Allow adequate time for deeper engagement—depth over breadth.

2. Read entire books—engage more profoundly with the research.

3. Respect the moral capacity of young people—strive for a citizenship effect.

4. One size doesn't fit all in cultivating or discovering strengths.

5. Humanize a topic by making a personal connection with anyone engaged in it.

6. Relevant learning sticks and feeds passions.

7. It's ok to change your mind.

8. Not someday, but now.

9. Create content and share it with an authentic audience.

10. Share stories and practice telling them.

11. Speak the language of passion—adjust your vocabulary.

12. Practice effective reflection.

1. Allow Adequate Time for Deeper Engagement—Depth Over Breadth

Matt Cone learned that by focusing on one big topic, like the history of Haiti or strategies aimed at poverty alleviation, rather than skipping around and trying to cover many disparate units, students could immerse themselves in various aspects of an issue, begin to appreciate its complexities, and start to see themselves as subject experts. By spending a few weeks or months on a big issue, students began to gravitate to particular interests, building relationships with other students or leaders in the field, and thinking more profoundly about problems they wanted to tackle. When in-class time didn't allow for the deep dive, Matt led a Global Poverty Reading Group before school, which students eagerly attended promptly at 7 a.m.

Another example of allowing for adequate time is found at the Science Leadership Academy (SLA), a magnet public high school in Philadelphia. The school is built around nurturing a long-term, inquiry-driven learning process. The structure of each school day reflects this, as does the organization of each academic year. Longer class periods are designed to allow for more laboratory work and performance-based learning in all classes, as well as hands-on experiences outside the building for upper grades. Classes aren't siloed by topic; rather, they are organized around big themes such as identity (Grade 9), systems (Grade 10), and change (Grade 11). These in turn serve three essential questions that form the basis of instruction: "How do we learn?" "What can we create?" and "What does it mean to lead?" So, the time each day, accumulating each year, feeds a passion discovery and building process that accumulates over 4 years of high school.

2. Read Entire Books—Engage More Profoundly With the Research

As Matt Cone began to hone his methods, he realized that students weren't expected to read entire books in their other classes and they were skipping from short articles to textbook citations to whatever bubbled to the top of their Internet search results. Students missed out on a deeper learning experience and, in effect, it seemed they weren't respected enough to be offered an actual book. One of Cone's students, Ashish Premkumar, a 2013 Boston University medical school graduate, credits the experience of staying up all night at age 15 to read Tracy Kidder's *Mountains Beyond Mountains*, about the work of Dr. Paul Farmer, among his most important formative experiences, leading to an outstanding career in global health (Friday, 2013). By contrast, other students, when probed, admitted to never having read a full book on their own in high school. Matt Cone learned that expecting students who didn't have academic confidence or role models to read an entire nonfiction title was unrealistic, so they spent class time reading books by global thought leaders together, aloud. Kidder's *Mountains Beyond Mountains* offers a compelling glimpse of anthropology, history, economics, and global health issues, within a hero's biography. Dan Ariely's *Predictably Irrational: The Hidden Forces That Shape Our Decisions* and Jeffrey Sachs' *The End of Poverty* provide a deeper sense of behavioral economics and macroeconomic strategies. These works represent some of the books that Cone's students have read as a class, which serve as guiding texts for deeper inquiry.

3. Respect the Moral Capacity of Young People—Strive for a Citizenship Effect

As Matt Cone sees each year, young people are fundamentally moral or ethical— they want to do good, to be part of something bigger than themselves. They don't need to be tricked into caring about important issues through gimmicks or prizes. Respect for students' capabilities helps Cone build students' academic confidence. He aims for a "citizenship effect," in which students will make an impact on something for which they have a passion. There is also a clear academic boost: Students often leave the class knowing a topic, like the history of Haiti, much more fluently and thoroughly than even U.S. history, a subject they are more traditionally taught. After taking Cone's class, almost every student takes honors and Advanced Placement classes in subsequent years.

> Young people are fundamentally moral—they want to do good, to be part of something bigger than themselves.

This idea is echoed by the SLA's founding principal, Chris Lehmann, in his 2011 TEDxPhilly talk:

> If we train kids to be workers, that's what we get . . . But if we shoot for citizenry as our goal, to help kids realize themselves in a world, in a community, then we will also get the husbands and wives, and fathers, and scholars, activists, community members, and friends that we need. Don't let anyone tell you that the purpose of school is working; the purpose is to learn how to live. And that makes all the difference in the world.

Both of these approaches imply a profound respect at the foundation of their interactions with students, another recurring theme in which student passions are encouraged to thrive.

4. One Size Doesn't Fit All in Cultivating or Discovering Strengths

Each student in Matt Cone's class chose a different topic to cover in his or her deep learning process. As it turns out, student choice offered a path toward finding strengths. Group work can also highlight the different strengths individuals have for completing a complex product, by encouraging those with a comparative advantage (e.g., organizing, puzzle-solving, speaking with many people, drawing, or performing physical activity) to build on their strengths and outsource their weaknesses. Opportunities and safety for trial and error also helped students discover where their strengths lay. Unlocking strengths and discovering passions proved infectious—peers began to see how they could do the same, although each individual's process would be different.

A few strategies for differentiated strength-finding include the following:

- *Be on the lookout for unique interests or qualities.* From a very early age, a child's particular preference for matching accessories or colors could signal a sensibility for design; one who seeks out patterns whether driving down the highway or noticing cracks in the sidewalk may have a particular aptitude for math. What may seem like quirks at an early age may signal passions later on. To help students begin to identify a major or career path, some college counselors have framed the question this way: "What did you always have to be told to stop doing when you were a kid?"

- *You don't know what you don't know.* If children haven't been exposed to the idea that they all possess unique talents and the various forms in which these talents can be expressed in future careers (e.g., a botanist, fundraiser, pastry chef, rocket scientist, orchestra conductor, adoption counselor, large animal veterinarian, food pantry logistics organizer), they won't be able to aspire to one of these vocations. Exposure to diverse possibilities through literature, movies, human interest news stories, and real people engaged in the work helps open the mind to solving more problems and imagining one's place in the world.

- *Be flexible, even after strengths have been identified.* Labeling a child as an artist, geek, nurturer, and so forth can prove counterproductive. Children will inevitably change their mind about their preferences and develop new strengths over time. Knowing that their interests are naturally fluid can be liberating, enabling children to try new activities and build new strengths. When children feel labeled, even in a positive way, this can weigh down their options later in life when career choices are crucial.

5. Humanize a Topic by Making a Personal Connection With Anyone Engaged in It

Matt Cone asks his students to seek out experts they might want to hear from. By outsourcing to thought leaders in the relevant fields, Cone accomplished two goals: (1) obtaining subject area guides with first-hand knowledge, and (2) putting a face and heart to the big issues students were exploring. This humanization of each topic helped create a sense of possibility in students. By speaking to people ranging from the director of a local nonprofit working on homelessness to the president of the World Bank, students met real people making a difference and thus felt less overwhelmed by global issues. Indeed, activists and experts served as a great source of hope for the students: Real people they got to know were working on real solutions.

> [Cone] had his students seek out experts they would want to hear from . . . activists and experts served as a great source of hope for the students: Real people they got to know were working on real solutions.

Students discovered that world-famous authorities enjoyed interacting with them, especially when they had done the work of seriously considering the issue and when they asked sincere and probing questions. Experts also need to experience hope for the future—hope that these passionate students could offer. In this way, the interaction became reciprocal, like a real relationship. The first expert approached by Matt's class was Dr. Paul Farmer. This served as a big turning point in learning for both students and teacher. In 2004, after reading *Mountains Beyond Mountains* about Dr. Farmer's work and circumstances in Haiti, the students huddled around a speakerphone to speak with him. Dr. Farmer read and responded to the journals of every single student. After meeting Dr. Farmer, the students were motivated to become more like him—dogged, determined, knowledgeable, caring, and compassionate. This led to students recruiting their friends, involving the wider community in their learning and activism, as well as raising substantial funds for Haiti. Since that time, technology has advanced significantly, so students are blogging, Skyping with experts, setting up Google Hangouts, making their own videos, following experts on social media (e.g., Twitter, Facebook, and Instagram), setting up their own Twitter accounts to spread the word on causes they care about, and sharing the work on YouTube for a global audience. Matt Cone makes sure that every student conducts a phone interview with his or her chosen expert, as engaging in the conversation remains a key skill; however, the range of communication platforms after the initial contact can reflect a wide variety of personality types, preferences, and strengths.

In a video called "Follow Your Passion," Rory Newcomb (2014) of Bombay offers yet another angle on humanizing learning: "Surround yourself with people who are amazing in ways that you are not, steal like an artist, and seek out resources from a Passionate Learning Network to overcome your limitations."

6. Relevant Learning Sticks and Feeds Passions

Students voluntarily seek cognitively complex learning when it helps solve problems that they care about. Material isn't forced down just in case it may be needed one day; rather, knowledge is thirstily sought, just in time, because it matters. Many of Matt Cone's students had not been considered the strongest academically, but the quality of their work ended up being more complex than what was taking place in honors classes they were deemed not ready for.

> Many of Matt Cone's students had not been considered the strongest academically, but the quality of their work ended up being more complex than what was taking place in honors classes they were deemed not ready for.

Relevance doesn't only take place in the arena of solving global problems. Other examples include the following:

- Third graders can demonstrate their reading fluency to first graders by reading a favorite story to them. Preparing to read to an authentic audience helps strengthen reading skills, cultivating a passion to read.
- When Rory Newcomb in Bombay found that the content in the QuizUp app was too rudimentary for her IB biology students, she contacted the game developers in Iceland and, along with her students, created IB-level biology content with over 500 questions that have now become part of the app. Studying for their biology test translated into creating a product for other students, compelling them to learn the material more deeply.

7. It's Ok to Change Your Mind

Matt Cone serves as a curator, guide, and mentor in a longer process and will often ask students the following question in the midst of their studies on a big issue: "What have you changed your mind on?" This signals an expectation that an open mind is vital and that change is an inevitable part of the learning and growth process. This is in line with Carol Dweck's pioneering work, which found that individuals with a growth mindset "believe that a person's true potential is unknown (and unknowable), that it's impossible to foresee what can be accomplished with years of passion, toil, and training" (Kelley & Kelley, 2013, citing Dweck, 2007). In other words, through effort and experience, we grow and change and have capabilities to pursue our passions; we aren't stuck within predetermined limitations.

Amid this dynamic development, the role of the adult guide is vital. Adults can help develop strengths from among shifting interests, whether by asking guiding questions, being transparent about their own learning processes, helping to curate material that probes more deeply into various aspects of a topic of interest, encouraging experimentation and rebounding from failure, or exploring new topics. Guidance can also offer reassurance that shifting interests and passions characterize healthy stages of a growth mindset.

8. Not Someday, But Now

Matt Cone's students inevitably gain a sense of urgency as they interact and delve into global challenges. When passions are stoked, students don't mind coming to school at 7 a.m. or staying up all night to read a book. As Chris Lehmann (2011) posed in his TEDxPhilly talk: "What if we stopped saying you'll need this someday? The lives you live matter now." Creativity gurus David Kelley and Tom Kelley (2013) cite the work of game designer Jane McGonigal, who coined the term *urgent optimism* as a vital stage in the process of gaining courage to be creative. Urgent optimism is "the desire to act immediately to tackle an obstacle, motivated by the belief that you have a reasonable hope of success. Gamers always believe that an 'epic win' is possible—that it is worth trying, and trying now, over and over again. In the euphoria of an epic win, gamers are shocked to discover the extent of their capabilities" (Kelley & Kelley, 2013, p. 47). The euphoria cited here evokes a profound state of passionate expression that, once realized, demonstrates capabilities far greater than ever anticipated.

9. Create Content and Share It With an Authentic Audience

Matt Cone realized early on that students' passion for the subject and their desire to produce high-quality work grow markedly when they are asked to create products (that demonstrate learning) for an authentic audience beyond the classroom. At the end of a unit, students are asked to create a poster and invite ten to fifteen people to view the presentation. This exercise has grown from an audience of ninety people to 350 people who come to see the academic posters and listen to students making a case for the serious issues they care about and arguing for their proposed solutions. Audience members include city council members, the superintendent of schools, professors from nearby University of North Carolina and Duke University, as well as family and friends. As Matt describes, "the night of presentations is almost like an explosion of their learning." For most of the students, it's the first time their learning has gained an audience beyond their teacher or parents, and they gain a sense of respect they've never felt before. Sharing learning that matters serves as a simple, natural step in a continuum of students developing passions and realizing themselves as authentic agents in changing the world. In an entrepreneurial context, presentations can be structured like a "pitch" to investors, in which the most compelling information is conveyed in the most effective format.

10. Share Stories and Practice Telling Them

Translate passions into real stories of real people, events, scientific discoveries, or products and take turns telling them. Not all students are storytellers, so offering diverse options on how to communicate ideas, from representing them with simple sketches, to creating films and games, allows for further development of entrepreneurial learners. Students don't want to mess up in front of their peers and respected experts, so they themselves raise the bar in terms of expectations when telling their stories publicly. Human stories bring academic subjects to life. As Matt learned, "Kids can't wrap their brains around macroeconomics, but they can relate to someone dying over not having $250 for a fistula surgery—the result of poor macroeconomic conditions."

11. Speak the Language of Passion—Adjust Your Vocabulary

Setting up students for a growth mindset and cultivating their passions is possible through the words that are used every day. Matt Cone prepares his students to build "expertise"; they gain fluency in anthropology, behavioral economics, and international development (depending on the focus of study that term), whereas previously they scarcely understood what these words even meant.

Among younger students, simple alterations to your own vocabulary and speaking style can make a difference. For example, rather than offering general praise and noticing inherent qualities, make it specific and point out effort. Change "You're so bright." or "You're so good at math." to specific "I" phrases, such as "I notice how hard you worked on your math facts. You've mastered adding two-digit numbers." Also including easy-to-remember and easy-to-get-excited-about terms—such as *Genius Hour* (more on this below) or *Passion Time*, as Illinois fifth-grade teacher Paul Solarz (2014) does (personal communication, August 21, 2014)—or words like *expert*, *discovery*, and even *strengths* and *virtues* launches a process that can transform a mindset toward possibilities and away from deficits.

12. Practice Effective Reflection

The final step, building reflection into the learning process, may be the most critical, as well as the most overlooked. This is where change, growth, resilience, empathy, humility, self-awareness, gratitude, and active listening get their heft and can help build lasting passions. Reflection goes hand in hand with intentionality and mindful learning.

One way that Matt Cone's classes engage in reflection is by writing thank-you letters to people that contributed to their project. In particular, a small group of students from a non-honors class was invited to travel across the country to meet a prominent philanthropist. Matt had these students write the philanthropist letters that went beyond usual thank-you notes; instead, students were to offer a sense of how they had grown from the experience.

The connection between intentionality, mindfulness, and reflection can begin in the youngest grades, such as during show-and-tell or on field trips. For example, show-and-tell can serve as a platform to begin sharing passions and interests, using storytelling. Take time to reflect at the end of this simple activity for students to note what interested them in their sharing choice: Did they recognize patterns or would they like to present something different or differently? Guiding questions are important prompts for active reflection.

WORK WITH WHAT YOU HAVE: SCENARIOS FOR IMPLEMENTING PASSION-BASED LEARNING

A year-round, student-driven, creative, encouraging environment offers an ideal setting for passion-based learning, yet we realize that not all schools can offer each of these elements. Creative educators have found workarounds that offer a quality experience despite limitations. Gradual implementation of passion-based learning can be implemented at a beginner, intermediate, or advanced level. Note that these categories are not fixed but fluid. For example, the strategy "use journaling deliberately, to reflect on strengths" serves as a good beginner activity, but it can easily become an "expanding" advanced implementation step if the district or school makes a commitment to building this writing and communication skill as part of the passion-building culture it has committed to, helps teachers cultivate this skill through targeted professional development, and expands on strengths identified through journaling by offering opportunities to translate reflection into action.

Thinking About

Beginning Activities for Implementing Passion-Based Learning

- *If you have one hour, try a Genius Hour.* The Genius Hour stems from corporate practices such as "20% Time" at Google and "FedEx Days" at FedEx, which set aside an hour or a day per week to encourage employees to work on new ideas or master new skills. By virtue of its very name, some may object that this tool remains on the sidelines, rather than front and center (see Hoffman, 2014). The autonomy has proven to be a way to prime passions among classrooms that have tried this tool. As teacher Gallit Zvi (2012) describes:

> Genius Hour is a precious time, loved by all my students. It is when they are allowed to develop their own inquiry question about whatever it is that they want to explore. They are then given about 3 one-hour Genius Hour sessions and then they are usually ready to present their learning to the class. Genius Hour is an amazing time. All the kids are excited and this creates a buzz in the air! Some students are huddled around a laptop doing research on countries they are interested in, others are creating websites, PowerPoints, and slideshows on an area of interest, and some are out in the hallway filming movies. Some aren't using technology at all, but rather are building and creating things with their hands. But no matter what they are working on, the common thread is that it is something they are interested in and/or passionate about.

This isn't always smooth sailing, so turning to support from the professional learning network #geniushour on Twitter can serve as a helpful community in which to exchange ideas. Check out the terrific clearinghouse of web resources on Genius Hour curated by Jerry Blumengarten (@cybraryman1) for more experiences.

- *Use journaling deliberately, to reflect on strengths.* A typical journaling activity can transform into a deliberate strength- and passion-finding exercise, with some mindful guidance. Use questions to spur the process.
  - Can you remember three recent experiences or occasions that brought you happiness? What do they have in common? How did you show your happiness?
  - What do you do that keeps your attention the longest? What do you often have to be told to stop doing before dinner, homework, school, or anywhere you need to be?

(Continued)

(Continued)

- o Do you think you are generous? Helpful? Kind? How do you show this?
- o Do you make people laugh? Talk? Become friends? Can you give examples?

As you begin sharing journaling prompts, you will get to know students better; their reflections on their interests will help them identify strengths, and your own guiding questions can become more refined along the way.

Implementing

Intermediate Activities for Implementing Passion-Based Learning

- *Make the most of recess and other "free" or "play" time.* Freeing up unhurried time in the day for boredom, play, or discovery helps children find their passions, as Tony Wagner argues in *Creating Innovators* (2012). Taking a reflective walk serves as a favored way to stoke creativity. Thought leaders from Richard Louv (*Last Child in the Woods*, 2008) to David Kelley and Tom Kelley (*Creative Confidence*, 2013) advocate a good walk not just to clear one's head but to also help spark ideas that matter.
- *Dedicate regular class periods over the school year to SOLEs.* Self-organized learning environments (SOLEs) are an initiative of the School in the Cloud (www.schoolinthecloud.org) that aims to spark creativity, curiosity, and wonder in students and inspire them to take control of their own learning. SOLEs are the brainchild of Professor Sugata Mitra, who conducted the famous "Hole in the Wall" experiment in a New Delhi slum in 1999. These experiments have revealed that groups of students can learn almost anything by themselves, given access to information (usually an Internet connection) and the ability to work as a community (Mitra, 2010). After the 1999 experiment, Professor Mitra received the prestigious $1 million TED Prize in 2013, with the aim of reinventing learning to become a child- and curiosity-centered experience.

○ The research and programmatic benefits of the TED Prize can be seized by teachers anywhere, as Joseph Jamison's fifth-grade classroom in New Jersey showed us. Jamison simply found out about Professor Mitra's education vision through his TED talk, got inspired, reached out via Twitter, and took initiative on his own to conduct a SOLE, tapping in to free resources from the School in the Cloud. Two years into the experiment, which is a learning process for the students as well as teachers and administrators, Mr. Jamison's class joined a global network of self-directed learners in the United Kingdom, India, and Ghana, with "Skype Grannies," or mentors who help guide inquiry via Skype from around the world. Questions or topics that open the research in Jamison's class have ranged from "The rights of the individual should be the primary object of all governments." to "What inventions have had the biggest impact on how we live?" (A bank of questions is available for anyone who creates a SOLE profile on the School in the Cloud website.) Students are eager for the unveiling of the question, then immerse themselves in the open-ended research, and, finally, share a presentation at the end of the hour with the entire class. It's not expected that students arrive at one correct answer, source, or presentation style. As students learn how to learn and teachers cede some of their control of class content and work, observers have also noted that kids who may have had learning or disciplinary challenges feel respected and empowered through this active approach to learning, causing a significant decline in corrective actions, and generally, passions are sparked for everyone engaged in this learning experience.

- *If you have 1 to 4 weeks, try a "January Term."* The Episcopal Academy is a college-preparatory independent school in Newtown Square, Pennsylvania, with high achievement expectations. School leaders seeking to implement out-of-the-box innovations knew that whatever they would propose to teachers who prided themselves on rigorous academics and traditional results needed to be strategically thought through and carefully planned. After 3 years of development, the Episcopal Academy rolled out their January Term, or JTerm program, a 2-week, immersive, cross-disciplinary learning experience for all students in Grades 9–12. JTerm courses ranged from "Designing Sacred

(Continued)

(Continued)

Spaces" to social and economic considerations of the restaurant and food industry, "Living and Dying in the USA" (a look at end of life issues), robotics, app development, game design, and immersion in the social, political, environmental, and economic life in places ranging from India to Panama. For a list of topics, see the Episcopal Academy 2013–2014 JTerm Course Guide in the Resources section.

- o Thanks to strong collaboration between teachers with varied skills sets but overlapping interests, parents who lent their professional expertise, and students who had the freedom to choose any topic they wished, without negative ramifications on grades, college admissions, or other commitments, the two-week JTerm translated into a deep-dive in passion-based learning. As a teacher commented, "When you tell teenagers they have to eat, you know something magical is happening." Another testimony to the power of passion-based learning is the fact that it couldn't be contained within the designated time and space, and a cultural shift at the tradition-based, preK–12 school began. For example, elementary and middle schoolers sometimes served as focus groups, audiences, or product testers, and they in turn began to discuss their own passions to pursue when they get to participate in JTerm; teachers were percolating about how they can inject other passions and cross-disciplinary topics in their general class time; and students considering life after high school began to open up to new possibilities for their own futures, having a better sense of their own strengths and interests.

- *Dedicate one "specials" class, if possible.* Lou Lahana is the middle school "techbrarian" (technology/library science specialist) at the Island School, P.S. 188, in Lower Manhattan, New York. His inquiry-based, trial-and-error experience and passion for social justice share many similarities with Matt Cone's. At the start of his attempting to connect with what mattered to students, Lou introduced them to a variety of technologies in the media center, and students worked on them for the sake of learning the various tools. But as he observed students' curiosity and desire to apply their learning, Lou began to find ways for the technology to be of service to students developing their passions around larger local and global challenges, rather than have the technology as the focal point of the class.

○ "Core" classes at the school don't offer much leeway in terms of personalized learning, so Lou makes the most of the two classes per cycle students spend with him. A key learning for him has been to loosen his control of the class: He removed the word "assignment" in favor of a series of possibilities and prompts. He then removed the rigid chronological lesson planning and instead exposed students to problems and had them choose one and create solutions or products to address it. Through careful research and planning, Lou honed his own job down to 3 minutes every morning to expose students to a particular issue. If it turns out that the issue is a student's interest, Lou has more in-depth information available on his class website (techbrarian.com; see the "Problems" tab) that would in turn serve as a basis for something the students would need to produce and dive into more deeply. Lahana evolved into a curator of resources. He found technology tools and content that aligned with students' passions and interests. As products began to roll in, a whole different dynamic around learning, motivation, identity, and confidence was created. Even evaluation altered to reflect this new way of working. On the bottom of the techbrarian. com "Problems" page, you'll see five questions (e.g., "Why are the solutions already out there not good enough?"). If students can answer these questions, backed up by experience and research on their particular issue, then they demonstrate their learning.

Expanding

Advanced Activities for Implementing Passion-Based Learning

- *Establish meaningful before- or after-school programs.* In a short video shot by students during their unforgettable visit, World Bank President Jim Kim (2013) praised Carrboro High School's Global Poverty Reading Group, the before-school club cited earlier, as "one of the most thoughtful and committed groups of young people I've ever seen." Organizations like Expanded Learning offer a network and

(Continued)

(Continued)

resources to build an after-school program specifically designed to spark passions in students. Destination Imagination, MOUSE Squad, Maker Ed, and Edutopia's resource round-up on after-school learning can offer programmatic guidance for out-of-school time that can build strengths and spur passions in students—possibly even serving as a demonstration for in-school innovations.

- *Establish a meaningful culminating project.* The Capstone Consortium is a national network of high schools implementing Capstone projects. In Capstone projects, students conduct long-term independent academic research that culminates in a formal presentation to a public audience. These projects have proven to cultivate student passions, in addition to being the focus for deeper learning of complex issues. Acknowledging that we remember 5% of what we hear, but 85% of what we teach, the Capstone project gets students to teach or demonstrate to others something about which they are truly interested. The Thacher School in Ojai, California, established the Capstone Consortium, which offers a professional learning community for any interested school (public, private, charter, or parochial) and a week-long summer professional development program for teachers.

At Rutland High School, a public school in rural Vermont, "Senior Inquiry Project" teacher and program coordinator Jen Kravitz found that the biggest challenge with the Capstone project was getting students to identify a genuine interest that they would want to commit months of work on. Ms. Kravitz served as an encouraging guide, creating a website that broke down a curriculum (see the Resources section) for every week, with guiding questions, milestones, inspiration, exercises to spur creativity, research tools, blogging guidelines, detailed expectations for clear evaluation (including the demonstration of global competency on any topic), and space for students to share their work. Topics ranged from "Society and Narcissism" to "Organized Crime" and "Alternative Energy." One suggestion we would add to this process is to search for ways to include a more authentic audience, so that the culmination isn't simply a presentation to a school audience but is a useful initiative that involves some form of action.

OVERCOMING CHALLENGES

Many, perhaps too many, members of the "boomerang genera-tion" described at the start of this book, not to mention many adults well into middle age, are still trying to figure out "what they want to be when they grow up." Finding our passions and acting on them is difficult if we're not sure what this looks like or how it's achieved in practice. Other challenges exist, a few of which we discuss below.

- *Misconception:* "Outsourcing" weakness in the class-room does not mean copying work, avoiding mastery, or remaining inside one's comfort zone. For example, if teams are engaged in conducting a KivaU lesson in math class, the person interested in researching the Malawian politics and social setting can "teach" his or her expertise to the rest of the team members, who are calculating the threshold for return on investment, legal requirements in Malawi for a women's microen-terprise, marketing considerations and strategy, climatic change and drought factors, and so on. Like a business team, each team member will be responsible for giving the entire "pitch" and knowing the material, even if he or she hasn't done all of the development. The team members "own" the entire enterprise, even if politics or meteorology isn't their particular interest.
- *Myth:* Passion-based learning is not rigorous enough. When a student likes what they are working on, it doesn't mean they are taking the easy way out. Indeed, because the student's interests are sparked, he or she can be guided to dig deeper into material and be chal-lenged around a topic, discipline, or methodology with which they might have been comfortable.
- *Myth:* Finding passions isn't feasible or appropriate for younger learners. Actually, it might be easier with elementary kids, as the wonder of discovery remains strong and they've had fewer academic pressures or

less discouragement or experience online "googling" answers to any question. It's important at the younger ages to allow room for changing interests.

- Scaling is challenging. When Matt Cone has each of his twenty-eight students convey an oral story around the complexities of the issue they took on, he makes a commitment to spending more time thinking about the work outputs of each student. If multiple classes engage in personalized work, he realizes the difficulty of grading and listening to so many oral presentations. This is one of the reasons for cultivating an authentic audience, so that the entire burden of assessing the product doesn't fall on one teacher.

- Classes that encourage students to take on passion projects may remain isolated from the more serious course content that shows up on tests. This is a reality that calls for leadership from the top, encouraging teachers to collaborate and offering professional development and organizational time to integrate this meaningful learning into the broader school day.

- Avoid labeling students if they find their strength or passion. If a student is a talented dancer, this is not mutually exclusive of writing or computational ability. They may gain confidence from their dancing but do not need to be boxed into a mindset such as "I'm a dancer, so I can't do/am not interested in math." Encourage intersections between strengths. For example, gaining experience on dance forms in various countries and writing about this or studying the physiology of dance, or even patterns and geometry of diverse choreography styles, can cultivate passions and build broader intellectual strengths.

REFLECTION

When passions are brought out in learning environments, we see over and over again that students don't mind skipping meals, waking up very early, talking to strangers (the good kind), or sacrificing other comforts so they can work on something meaningful. As the examples in this chapter point out, finding one's own passions, let alone helping students tap into their own, rarely unfolds along a straight line. The process is fraught with trial and error, or what some might regard as failure. Once you are aware that the road is thorny, then you are on the lookout for challenges and are more patient in the face of them. You know they'll come along; you persevere, try and try again, and give yourself a longer timeline. The culture of learning changes as a result.

Finding passions is like developing a muscle; building empathy is similar. The more the muscle is exercised, the more likely it will be demonstrated. Without nurturing, honing, and recognizing this ability, it atrophies. Here are some questions for you to consider:

- What sorts of activities will you engage in, and encourage for others, to build your strength in finding your passion? To nurture that strength in your students?
- What passions do you possess that you can model to your students so that by your example they can cultivate their own passions?
- Identify some times when you will need to step back as an instructor so that students have the space they need to discover on their own.
- List some ways in which you might take a more active role as a mentor, guide, curator, or instigator.

ACTIVITY #1: CONDUCT A SOLE TO GET DEEPER ABOUT YOUR PASSIONS

Participants

Educators and/or students

Objective

Participants will experience a SOLE, or self-organized learning environment, in order to put into practice many of the principles of passion-based learning, such as depth over breadth, striving for a "citizenship effect" or caring about important issues, respecting different approaches that various learners may take, and so on, into their own learning process. SOLEs are created when educators encourage kids (or each other) to work as a community to answer their own vibrant questions by using the Internet. Through this effort, they will experience the freedom and independence to traverse learning paths of their own choosing in pursuit of a solution to a driving question and to help discover or reinforce topics around which they feel passionate.

Materials

- Internet-enabled device for conducting research
- Notebook for ideation
- Large screen for sharing findings with a group (optional)

Process

SOLEs are traditionally conducted in small groups of about four people; yet in this case, participants can work on their own if the driving question centers on an individual interest. A group will work if students are investigating larger social issues in which multiple people might share an interest. Participants can move around freely to see what breakthroughs others are having, talk and discuss among each other and across groups, and even change groups if they feel compelled to do so.

The process (approximately 1 hour total) is broken into the following three distinct parts, as suggested in the Sole Toolkit (http://www.ted.com/prize/sole_toolkit#):

1. *Inquiry:* Ask a driving question (see below for some suggestions) and explain the SOLE process. Generate interest by offering a creative prompt, like an image or video, or playing an audio clip that relates to the question. (5 minutes)

2. *Investigation:* Begin research, refine the collaboration process (groups will decide who will do what and how this contributes to answering the driving question), and take notes. (40 minutes)

3. *Review and reflect:* Organize how the learning/findings will be shared; create an informal presentation (this can get more elaborate with experience, more time, or depending on strengths and objectives of the group. For example, findings can be shared in the form of a photo essay, watercolor painting, graphic/comic depiction, skit, PowerPoint presentation, or TED-style talk). For the purposes of this initial 1-hour exercise, a facilitated discussion asks participants to share how the process unfolded, surprises they encountered, lessons on research and collaboration, and, importantly, if they found they gravitated to particular issues during the investigation process (following a simple presentation of key points is likely all that can be conveyed in the allotted time).

Possible driving questions for discovering/cultivating passions: Some possible questions include the following (note that each of these calls for research as well as probing and honing one's own interests):

- What is the most urgent issue that world leaders should come together to solve?
- If you owned a Google Self-Driving Car and Google Glass, how would you use them on the weekends?
- What was the most important invention from the first half of the 20th century?
- What is the most significant design movement?
- If you had a day to spend at one of the seven ancient or modern Wonders of the World, with an unlimited budget, where would it be, and how would you spend your day, given the unique circumstances of that location?

Reflection

Some examples of reflective questions are as follows:

- After experiencing the SOLE, how comfortable did you feel conducting open-ended research on open-ended questions?
- Would you take this activity and SOLE method to your own students? How much direction would you want to give them and how involved in the investigation would you get?

Take a risk and try it in your classroom! This could be well suited at the start of a new unit or shortly after a few key concepts have been introduced. Or, learn simply for the sake of learning and experiencing a SOLE, and try one of the questions provided at the School in the Cloud website (http://www.theschoolinthecloud.org).

ACTIVITY #2: TAKE A PURPOSEFUL WALK OUTSIDE

Silicon Valley walking meetings and even negotiations by the likes of Steve Jobs, Mark Zuckerberg, and countless others have passed beyond the stuff of legends to become an accepted practice among innovators who prefer to get outdoors, actively moving their bodies while stimulating thoughts. Education influencers like Harvard's Tony Wagner advocate a process of *play* to help find *purpose* that ultimately leads to discovering *passions*. And Paul Salopek, the Pulitzer Prize winning journalist, has embarked on a 7-year Out of Eden walk across the planet to uncover the stories of our times at a pace of 3 miles per hour, inviting anyone who likes to join him by walking in their own communities, discovering hidden wonders that lie in our midst, or under our feet, or above our heads.

Objective

Purposefully observe details in your familiar environment by getting outside, taking a walk, and noticing how something seen outside might be a metaphor for something you are experiencing in your own life or for which you feel passionate about.

Materials

Wear comfortable clothing and walking shoes, and take something to record observations with (but make sure your recording device will not distract you from walking; e.g., if you are taking notes on your smartphone, turn off the sound completely so you are not taking phone calls or checking e-mail or social media). Because of the potential for distraction, a notebook and pen/pencil is the preferred form of recording ideas. Even the act of handwriting or sketching can serve as part of your mindful discovery process.

Process

(approximately 40 minutes total)

Walk alone to record personal observations and discover interests or details in the landscape.

- Introduce and share the objective of the walk. (4 minutes)
- Walk for 20 to 30 minutes. While walking, notice where your eyes are drawn to and how your body feels, and try to maintain a steady breath. What are you noticing now that you are not rushing or preoccupied with other matters?
- Write down reflections based on ONE of the following possible question prompts (10 minutes):
  - Take a moment to write down all that you see in one square foot of area where you are walking. You may need to bend down to ground level and look very closely. Imagine you are an ant hauling some of the stash found in that square of land. Write a paragraph from the ant's perspective.
  - Inspired by the Out of Eden Walk, what are natural or man-made boundaries that you observe on your walk? What purpose do they serve?

- Sketch an image—of anything—that you see on your walk.
- Write a poem based on this walk. (There are no boundaries to the poem or any other instructions—it can be as long, as literal, as ridiculous, as contemplative, or as free-form as you wish.)

Reflection

Share (privately in your journal or with the group) your reflections from the walk and the question that you considered during the walk. Does your choice of question or the way you answered it help reveal something about your interests and potential passions? What?

Next Steps

Try to repeat this purposeful walk with a question prompt on a regular basis over the course of the year (monthly? quarterly?) and look for patterns in your observations, writing, or interests. You can do this with colleagues, on your own, or with your students.

REFERENCES

Boss, S. (2013, November 27). In India, a school that empowers students and teachers. Retrieved September 25, 2014 from http://www.edutopia.org/blog/india-school-empowering-schools-teachers-suzie-boss.

Dweck, C. (2007). *Mindset: The new psychology of success.* New York, NY: Ballantine Books.

Fox, J. (2009, November 16). 10 tips for discovering your child's strengths. *Huffington Post.* Retrieved November 3, 2014 from http://www.huffingtonpost.com/jenifer-fox/10-tips-for-discovering-y_b_288460.html

Friday, L. (2013, June 6). An unconventional OB/GYN: New MED grad brings back lessons in global health from Lebanon. *BU Today.* Retrieved August 21, 2014, from http://www.bu.edu/today/2013/an-unconventional-ob-gyn/

Hoffman, S. (2014). No more Genius Hours, 20% Time or FedEx Days. *Findings in Research & Development*. Retrieved September 3, 2014, from http://blogs.asbindia.org/findings/2014/01/24/no-more-genius-hours-20-time-or-fedex-days/

Kelley, D. & Kelley, T. (2013). *Creative confidence: Unleashing the creative potential within us all*. New York, NY: Crown.

Kidder, T. (2004). *Mountains beyond mountains: The quest of Dr. Paul Farmer, a man who would cure the world*. New York, NY: Random House.

Kim, J. (2013). Harlem Shake, Carrboro High. Retrieved September 1, 2014, from http://youtu.be/GvkzKlJMQow

Lehmann, C. (2011). TEDxPhilly: Education is broken. Retrieved September 7, 2014, from http://youtu.be/tS2IPfWZQM4

Louv, R. (2008). *Last child in the woods: Saving our children from nature deficit disorder*. Chapel Hill, NC: Algonquin.

Mitra, S. (2010, July). TEDGlobal 2010: The child-driven education. Retrieved August 7, 2014, from http://www.ted.com/talks/sugata_mitra_the_child_driven_education?language=en

Newcomb, R. (2014). Follow your passion. Retrieved September 16, 2014 from http://youtu.be/Yr3VQgnNYsk

Solarz, P. (2014, August 21). Here are my Passion Time (Genius Hour) resources. Retrieved August 20, 2014, from http://psolarz.weebly.com/2013-2014-passion-projects.html

Wagner, T. (2012). *Creating innovators: The making of young people who will change the world*. New York, NY: Scribner.

Zvi, G. (2012). Integrating technology and Genius Hour: My journey as a teacher and learner. Retrieved September 16, 2014, from http://www.gallitzvi.com/home/what-is-genius-hour

RESOURCES

After-School Learning: http://www.edutopia.org/blogs/tag/after-school-learning

Business Strengths Finder for Kids: http://www.entrepreneurkidsacademy.com/wp-content/uploads/2014/01/Business-Strengths-Finder.pdf

This is a chart for helping students determine their personal interests and strengths, more specifically for entrepreneurial activity in kids. For teachers, try the Teaching Strengths Quiz located on the sidebar of this

article, to identify your own strengths (http://www.weareteachers. com/hot-topics/special-reports/teach-to-your-strengths).

Capstone Consortium: http://blogs.thacher.org/capstone/

Clearinghouse of Web Resources on Genius Hour: curated by J. Blumengarten (@cybraryman1)

Destination Imagination: http://www.destinationimagination.org/home/page-26

Episcopal Academy JTerm Course Guide 2013–2014: http://inside .episcopalacademy.org/drum/chall/JTerm_020513.pdf

Expanded Learning: http://www.expandinglearning.org/

Lou Lahana: http://www.techbrarian.com/2014/08/31/whats-your-problem/
Lahana is the technology coordinator at the Island School in New York City.

Maiers, A., & Sandvold, A. (2010). *The passion-driven classroom: A framework for teaching and learning.* New York, NY: Routledge.

Maker Ed: http://makered.org/

Mouse Squad: http://mousesquad.org/

Rutland High School Capstone Curriculum: http://rhscapstone .weebly.com/curriculum.html

School in the Cloud, Start Your SOLE Profile: https://www.the schoolinthecloud.org/coordinators/sign_up

Schoolwide Enrichment Model: http://www.gifted.uconn.edu/sem/
This website describes an approach for developing the strengths and talents of all students.

Skype Grannies: https://www.theschoolinthecloud.org/library/reso urces/being-a-skype-granny http://blog.ted.com/a-school-in-the-cloud-sugata-mitra-accepts-the-ted-prize-at-ted2013/

Zhao, Y. (2012). *World class learners: Educating creative and entrepreneurial students.* Thousand Oaks, CA: Corwin.

4

Curriculum Flexibility and Breadth

Personalization With the Common Core

by Kay Tucker

It has also been argued that the core curriculum only prescribes the essential knowledge and skills a child needs, thus it is not the ceiling, rather the floor. Unfortunately, due to the different status and stakes, the floor usually becomes the ultimate goal. This is what has been referred to as curriculum narrowing.

(Zhao, World Class Learners, *2012, p. 37)*

The Mosaic Collective, Castle Rock, Colorado

"The majority of high-school students are compliant and somewhat disengaged, with untapped reservoirs for deep learning," states Dr. James Calhoun, principal at Castle View High School (Reuter, 2014). Castle View High School is a large public high school in Douglas County, Colorado, with an enrollment of approximately 1,800 students in Grades 9–12. Agreeing with this statement and taking it on as a real-world challenge, Michael Schneider and Ryan McClintock set out to design a viable solution. They imagined a school setting that would "... attempt to create intrinsically motivated, goal oriented passionate students able to take full ownership of their education before they fully matriculate into the world of work or post-high school education" (Schneider, 2013).

Their vision eventually became a new academy, or "school within a school," called the Mosaic Collective. The academy focuses on inquiry-based learning and empowers students to build their own learning pathways based on personal interests and strengths. Students focus on doing and creating as learning. They learn as they design, build, experiment, produce, invent, and so forth. The confines of schedules and classrooms are removed, and students have weekly meetings with advisors and participate in group seminars and electives. "We purposefully removed barriers like bell schedules and just about anything that kind of boxes our students and their thinking in," says McClintock. Schneider adds, "You get a freshman who gets on his calendar, sends you an invite and tells you what room to be in and what time and what they need from you—talk about changing the complete paradigm of what education is—students telling their teachers, where to be, when to be there, and what they need from you while you are together" (Barber, 2014).

With a strong belief that motivation is at the core of learning, Dr. Calhoun trusts that in this paradigm, students' intellectual passions will ignite. He presents a plausible example of a teenage boy who loves to skateboard. This student's passion could become the centerpiece of a student-inquiry project and a springboard for the study of physics, science, and math; for product design and new material development;

or for petitioning the city council to build a skateboard park. Personal academic goals will be set, and an individualized curriculum will be established with the guidance and mentoring of content experts and advisors. After developing his ideas for a product or service solving a real-world problem or need, the skateboarder would defend the idea as well as persuade others of the value of his project. There would be multiple opportunities for feedback and revision.

This rigorous approval process for a student-inquiry project was created by Mosaic teachers and is called "project tuning." It includes expectations for the integration of multiple disciplines, guaranteeing a consistent quality of curriculum. The research and processes involved for students to create and actualize these authentic products or services will be strong proof of learning, and credits will be awarded in relation to typical defined course credits. Schneider sums up this philosophy for student-led learning as follows: "We need to . . . get students to take ownership of their learning . . . I don't mind telling them what they need to learn to get their diploma. But when they do it, how they do it, what books they read—I don't feel I have to tell them that" (Reuter, 2014). Similar principles exist among schools that are successful in creating a broad and flexible curriculum within the confines of defined national standards.

Principles for Creating a Broad and Flexible Personalized Curriculum While Covering Standards

The following main ideas are highlighted in this example and will be expanded on to demonstrate how they can be put into practice:

- Allow students to uncover curriculum as they solve real-world problems.
- Intentionally align student work to standards—then take it beyond the standards.
- Provide multiple opportunities for learning.
- Create opportunities for continual advisement and relationship building.

Allow Students to Uncover
Curriculum as They Solve Real Problems

(See Activity 1: Global Issues Create Opportunities for Learning)

Defined national standards are generally rooted in relevant real-world learning; however, to meet the needs of our "subject-driven" and "age-separated" school environments and testing requirements, these standards have been compartmentalized and pieced into small parts, so their relevance is diminished, particularly among students. Once these standards are "pulled apart,"teachers have worked in traditional models to merge the standards into integrated units in order to create more meaning for students and to be more efficient in teaching all standards across a limited time frame. The power of new models of instruction, like Mosaic, is that instead of teachers planning integrated units to "cover" curriculum, students are allowed to "uncover" curriculum as their individual inquiry process leads them down a naturally integrated path of learning.

When students analyze, evaluate, and create in unpredictable real-world situations, learning becomes both rigorous and relevant, mandating the use of higher-order thinking skills. The Rigor/Relevance Framework created by the International Center for Leadership in Education (ICLE) is designed to help teachers choose instructional strategies to attain high achievement and differentiation for all students. ICLE fuses a "thinking continuum" based on Bloom's Taxonomy with an "action continuum" created by Bill Daggett, to illustrate the power of what it means for students to reach a desired level of adaptation where students are able to think in complex ways. This high level of thinking and acting "signifies action—use of knowledge to solve complex, real-world problems and create projects, designs, and other works for use in real-life situations" (International Center for Leadership in Education, 2015). Getting students to this level of ability to act with agility and reason in unknown variable realities is a quality that is much sought after in today's job market, and it exceeds the boundaries of any defined set of standards or outcomes.

The Workshop School, a public school in the School District of Philadelphia, exemplifies this rigorous and relevant approach to learning. The school's website includes a tagline that states "Teaching Students to Change the World" and describes the school's mission to " . . . unleash the creative and intellectual potential of young people to solve the world's toughest problems. We do this by putting real world problems at the center of the curriculum, and evaluating students' work based on the progress they make in defining, exploring, and ultimately developing solutions to those problems" (Workshop School, 2015).

The following are some examples highlighted on the school's website, showing how the school's mission is exemplified in student projects.

- *818 Project:* Students and teachers worked in teams to design and build a biodiesel-powered sports car that could get 100 miles per gallon. They showed this car at the White House Maker Faire to an interested audience, including President Obama, Bill Nye, and Will.I.Am.
- *Land RAFTS:* Land RAFTS is the result of a challenge in The Workshop School's Sustainability Workshop to design projects that have an impact on the world. A group of students took on a project that revolved around their desire to solve a problem that became evident to them after the 2010 earthquake in Haiti. Even with the high level of aid to Haiti being provided by numerous countries, an inordinate amount of Haitians were left without homes and were living in temporary shelters. The students decided to design a better solution to the temporary housing and created highly efficient modular housing kits that could be transported in shipping containers and sent anywhere in the world after a disaster.

The students at The Workshop School created not only viable products but also ones that are needed. Without any additional intervention, their learning pathway naturally incorporated multiple content standards—the same standards that teachers need to assess. Going beyond the problem solving in typical math and science programs, the interconnectedness of the various fields of learning that are evident in this approach results in an increased potential of not only meeting standard expectations but exceeding them. As students dig deep for information and uncover facts and solutions, the work they do is both rigorous and relevant—students apply their learning and thinking to unknown situations in the real world. As Simon Hauger, principal and co-founder of The Workshop School, states in a video on the school's website: "If you want to do real work in the world, you have to be able to read, you have to be able to write, you have to be able to argue and back things up with facts" (Flick, 2014).

Intentionally Align Student Work to Standards—Then Take It Beyond the Standards

(See Activity 2: Intentionally Align Student Work to Standards)

Once a student decides on a real-world problem to drive inquiry, the next step is to define a learning pathway that provides the "need to know" information in order to solve the problem. It is the management of this path that becomes crucial. The intentional alignment of personalized, student-driven learning to required content is what allows educators to not only connect standards to relevant learning pathways but to also include opportunities for expanded thinking that goes beyond standards. There are a couple of strategies that work well for this approach, which can be flexible and yet deliberate in order to "meet standards" and even to exceed them.

Students as co-creators of their personalized curriculum: In a time of curriculum narrowing due to a focus on high-stakes testing and a one-size-fits-all approach, one of the biggest challenges that educators face is how to engage students to be excited and passionate about their learning and to understand that what they are learning is meaningful beyond the test.

Increasing attention is being given to providing opportunities for students to shape their learning—to be co-creators, co-producers, and co-designers of their learning. This is more than simply increasing participation in learning by allowing students to choose a textbook or co-design assessments or rubrics. Our discussion needs to move to how we authentically approach the co-creation of curriculum with students that also meets the expectations of national or common standards. Students may not have the ability or the expertise to design curriculum for current paradigms of education driven by one-size-fits-all standards. There is, however, evidence to support the fact that motivation influences learning as it promotes student engagement, and that students are more motivated to learn if they can make personal and relevant connections to their learning. This is why they need to be involved in co-designing their individual learning pathways.

Let's look at an example from Mapleton Early College (MEC) in Denver, Colorado, which is a combination of two high school models, Big Picture Learning and Early College. Students at MEC learn in a college-preparatory environment and combine classes with independent project-based learning based on their interests. They also participate in real-world learning through professional internships (Learning Through Internship or LTI). Central to their philosophy is that students will take an interest and turn it into deep learning and hard work. Take the example of one student who was interested in botany and science. With the help of his mentors/advisors, the student scripted his personal learning pathway and researched the flora of New Guinea in order to aid conservation efforts there. Within a framework of learning that embraces personalization, he created a broad and flexible curriculum that not only suited his needs but also allowed him to meet requirements for learning that can be applied to his future work in horticulture and genetics. The path he scripted prepared him for his LTI as a research assistant in the horticulture laboratory at the University of Denver, and he talks about it in the video called "A Big Picture Learning Student Talks About the Work at His LTI" (bplearning, 2008).

Creating a context for learning with a conceptual curriculum: Creating a context for learning is the same as setting the stage for learning, and it is important that this stage is rooted in real-world experiences and immerses the students in connected and conceptual thinking. This is what sparks their curiosity and leads students to question within a frame of reference. This frame of reference is one that is predetermined by teachers—one that will lead to an applied understanding of a concept. This is a viable strategy to use with younger students.

For example, sixth-grade students at Lone Tree Elementary School in Douglas County, Colorado, embarked on a journey of product-oriented learning. However, instead of a wide-open world of topics and possibilities, which might overwhelm students new to such a process, the teachers directed the learning based on intended outcomes in a standards-based environment. The statement, "The world is in our hands," became the context for learning. This also connected to their big picture conceptual curriculum based on the enduring understanding, "Interdependence impacts outcomes." Students were immersed in real-world settings, visuals, statements, and questions to provoke their thinking.

Some of the questions that drove individual inquiry in order to help motivate the students to conduct purposeful research and experimentation, and led to creative problem-solving, included the following:

- How do our decisions impact physical systems?
- How do our choices impact the environment?
- How does a changing environment impact us?
- How do our decisions help us become responsible members of a global society?

Students analyzed the cause and effect of global issues (deforestation, fracking, erosion, ice caps, climate change, pollution, etc.) as they answered their personal questions. They developed multiple ideas for products and services and presented their ideas to parents, peers, and real-world experts.

This authentic application of knowledge crossed multiple "required" content areas for their grade level. The teachers were impressed by the amount of information the students uncovered, claiming that they never would have thought to teach the students what they ultimately learned. This example demonstrates how product-oriented, student-driven curriculum actually results in more rigorous learning, even at a relatively young age. The role of teachers is vital here, to help spur inquiry, but teachers also recognize when to get out of the way for students to own and deepen their learning.

Provide Multiple Opportunities for Learning

Schools working successfully in this new paradigm are addressing the stipulation of a guaranteed curriculum by providing multiple opportunities for learning. With large blocks of time dedicated to independent and collaborative hands-on learning for individuals or teams, academic thinking is supported and enhanced with seminars, online learning, participation in traditional classes for certain subject areas, and connections to real-world experts.

Simon Hauger talks about student schedules at The Workshop School:

> Two-thirds of the day they have project blocks and the academics are integrated into the blocks. Seminars are content focused, but when they work well, they actually inform the projects. . . . we need to get rid of false academic distinctions. No one in real life says it's 8:54—now I'm doing Social Studies. . . . it's now 9:34—I am becoming a scientist. (Flick, 2014)

When teachers in the Mosaic program discover common needed content, they either create classes using Moodle, an open-source learning platform, or they set up seminars of choice. Students wanting to learn Spanish for real-world application scenarios either join other students for class or facilitate their own learning by online forums for learning language.

Michael Schneider confirms their goal of student empowerment combined with multiple opportunities for learning by saying:

> You get a freshman who gets on his calendar, sends you an invite and tells you what room to be in and what time and what they need from you—you talk about changing the complete paradigm of what education is. No longer does is it have to be one adult telling 30 kids what to do and when to do it and how to do it, but instead students telling their teachers where to be, when to be there, and what I need from you while we are together. (Barber, 2014)

Create Opportunities for Continual Advisement and Relationship Building

The value of personalized adult guidance in this new model of learning is no different than the value it has held over the years in any successful learning environment. Students excel in environments where they feel that someone cares for them, understands their passions, and supports them in their personal endeavors. Taking this to the next level for success means that our conversations have a different focus. Instead of working with students to make sure they obtain growth and learning within a model in which teachers assign tasks, the focus is on aligning student pathways with required outcomes.

"Discover Your Own Path" is the banner header for Jefferson County Open School (JCOS) (2015), an option school in Colorado. JCOS opened in 1970 and it is known for being a place where learners develop the skills and abilities of life-long learners. The JCOS staff members assess student learning in ways that challenge students to demonstrate personal, social, and intellectual growth. In a book written about JCOS, *Lives of Passion, School of Hope: How One Public School Ignites a Lifelong Love of Learning*, author Rick Posner talks about how this school has transformed the lives of many students and extended family members by personal empowerment and the development of confidence, curiosity, and compassion. The book relates stories and reflections of the school's alumni, their involvement in directing their own learning, and their success stories in finding a future career suited to them (Posner, 2009).

Scott Bain, principal of JCOS, created the Community "Owner's Manual" 2014–2015. In the following, Bain (2014) describes the primary role of teachers as advisors in this self-directed learning environment:

> At all levels students work closely with their advisor in the development of their personal curriculum. Both individually and in groups, advising is about developing strong, caring relationships between adults and students, and between students and students. JCOS is committed to preserving educational choices for all students and parents. In the face of increasing standardization, our emphasis on personal, social, and intellectual development helps to prepare students for an ever-changing world.

> The role of Advisor at the Open School is the most important responsibility for all teachers. As Advisors, teachers are student advocates and learning facilitators who assist students in setting and achieving the goals they set for their Goals/Individualized Education Plan (IEP). The Advising relationship is paramount in guiding students towards successful completion of all aspects of their program.

The role of advisors is further explained as Bain (2014) talks about the value of relationship building with students and their advisors:

> Advisors meet individually with each student on a regular basis to build the relationships necessary to guide students through their individualized program. Once a trusting relationship is established, Advisors can provide deep and meaningful feedback to assist each student in the creation of a challenging personal, social, and intellectual program.

Having systems in place for this purposeful goal setting analysis, planning, and alignment to curriculum is what guarantees success in a standards-driven system. As this example demonstrates, the role of adults/teachers is far from diminished; rather, it is reoriented for greater relevance in a knowledge-driven economy and world.

Provide Choice in Learning Options Within School Systems—An Academies Approach

Central to developing a climate and culture in our school systems that respects student choice and offers relevant learning opportunities is offering multiple options for both students and parents. From its' inception, Castle View High School was designed around choice for students. Mosaic (CV The Mosaic Collective, 2015) was added as an option to a list that already included the following:

- Biotechnology and Health Sciences Academy
- Leadership, Global Studies, and Communication Academy
- Science, Technology, Math and Engineering Academy
- Visual and Performing Arts Academy

As Michael Schneider states, "Mosaic is just the next level of the choice. . . . To us, it's the next logical step in that notion of moving from choice to true empowerment. Our job as teachers is to not put them into a box, but to craft the box that works best for the student" (Barber, 2014).

This "school within a school" approach of Mosaic is not the directive for all students, but it is offered as an option for those wanting to embark on a journey of student-directed curriculum, flexible schedules, and entrepreneurial thinking. Providing choice such as this alongside more traditional paradigms in education minimizes possible resistance from parents and other community members. It also provides opportunities for interest to be piqued as others watch the initial risk-takers test out new ideas.

Strategies for Creating a Broad and Flexible Personalized Curriculum While Covering Standards

In the Classroom

Make the Relevance and Application of Standards Visible

Make sure students understand the specific outcomes they are expected to achieve for the year or the class. Discuss the relevance and real-world application of these standards and engage in questioning about how the standards relate to other standards in real-world scenarios. Empower students to think about ways they could demonstrate their learning if they combined several desired outcomes in an integrated approach. Let students create their own thematic units that lead to relevant participation in actual realities.

Connect Standards to Current Happenings in the World

(See Activity 1: Global Issues Create Opportunities for Learning)

"Real Life Is Our Teacher" or "Learn for Life" could be classroom slogans. Make sure students are immersed in actuality and have the opportunity to connect the relevance of standards to their life. As educators we need to challenge ourselves to get out of the "bubble of curriculum" that keeps us tied to our classrooms and standards and create greater connections and opportunities for students. Designate time or areas in your class for "What on EARTH is happening?" or "What in the world is happening?" Focus on current events related to your outcomes and connect to or refer to the ever-changing data accessible in our digital world. Make the standards come alive in a way that piques students' curiosity and entices them to get involved and learn more about real life.

Create Systems for Students to Self-Document Individual Progress Toward Standards

(See Activity 3: Create Systems for Students to Self-Document Individual Progress Toward Standards)

Instead of teachers documenting student progress toward meeting a list of standards on a report card or progress report, consider putting systems in place for students to be in charge of this task. The process alone will create understanding and help students to be aware of situations that could be considered as opportunities to pursue as a means of demonstrating understanding. Allowing students the chance to demonstrate understanding of multiple outcomes, through one self-directed task, increases awareness of the personal relevance of standards.

At JCOS, the students in secondary grade levels create their own transcripts. The level to which this personalizes and creates relevance for their learning is vastly different than the traditional reporting out of standards for students. There is no doubt it could be considered more valuable.

> The culmination of each student's experience at the Open School is documented in the Final Transcript. Open School transcripts are written by the student and include a Personal Statement, class list, Advisor support letters, and a summary of each individual learning experience. Students include detailed information about knowledge and skills gained and what was of personal significance to the student. When a student includes an Open School class in his or her Transcript, this indicates that the student has met or exceeded all course requirements for that experience. Transcripts are authenticated by the student's academic Advisor, another faculty member familiar with the student's accomplishments, and the school Principal. The Transcript is the official record used for college and job applications. (Bain, 2014)

In the School

Create a Schoolwide Culture of
Personalized Learning Aligned With Outcomes

Adopt a philosophy of personalized learning with expanded opportunities for the entire learning environment. Using the following essential questions, it is possible to apply a common theme for not only students but for staff as well: How does inquiry create sustainable and personal learning? How do we become self-directed learners? How can we create opportunities for student/teacher ownership of their learning?

Modeling for teachers what is possible for them to do with students, Lone Tree Elementary School in Douglas County, Colorado, created and set into action a plan for personalized professional development. Each teacher self-directs their learning aligned to their professional growth plan and teachers are held accountable for their learning with the following sequence of assignments (the same sequence could be altered and used for students):

- Set personal goals.
- Create an action plan/learning pathway.
- Negotiate a schedule for completion based on available resources and extent of study.
- Implement and document how new strategies have been put into practice.
- Reflect on changed instructional strategies and how they impacted teaching and learning.
- Create a product/service that will be presented to an authentic audience.

Teachers also have professional digital portfolios where they document their teaching practice and growth and effectiveness as an educator. The correlation between teachers and students is based on the fact that both are evaluated on a set of outcomes and expectations for effective teaching and learning. It is awareness of these standards that enables teachers to effectively drive their learning, and awareness should also be given to students so that they may do the same.

Set Schoolwide Expectations for
Self-Directed Standards-Based Learning

Since its inception in 1970, JCOS has worked to create a school-wide system that empowers students, while at the same time holds them accountable for graduation expectations. Referring once again to the Community "Owner's Manual" 2014–2015, Bain (2014) defines each level of learning and sets a clear path of requirements to continue to the next. The following is what is expected for the Intermediate Area (IA), which is Grades 4 and 5.

In the IA, students work to develop the skills, attitudes, knowledge, and behavior necessary to be successful in a self-directed learning environment. IA expectations include the following:

Essential for Membership in the IA

- Have an advisor—a staff advocate.
- Have personal, social, and intellectual goals to guide learning.
- Complete learning activities and maintain portfolio documentation of personal, social, and intellectual growth.
- Be safe, kind, and appropriate.

To Be a Successful Member of the IA

- Be actively involved in the community, including the Advising and Community Circle.
- Maintain an organized portfolio documenting personal, social, and intellectual growth.
- Contribute (give as well as take) meaningfully to the Open School community at large.

Requirements for Continuation to Pre-Walkabout

- Successfully complete IA Trips.
- Successfully complete the Bridges class.
- Successfully complete a Self-Directed Voyage.
- Document learning in a Voyage presentation.
- In a portfolio, document significant personal, social, and intellectual growth to an appropriate level of proficiency, as agreed upon by the Advisor, Advisee, and Parent(s).

In the School System

Create Communities of Practice

Encourage school leaders or professional development teams to create Communities of Practice as a forum for exchanging ideas with a focus on increasing the breadth and flexibility of curriculum by personalizing learning, even within the confines of standards. Within Douglas County, Colorado, there is a group of district leaders who organized "Create Something Great: Ideate, Initiate, Implement." The Create Something Great Google+ Community (2015) describes the *why* behind this effort as " . . . an opportunity to empower educators, community members and industry to collectively transform the culture of American education by building common understandings, taking risks, designing specific solutions, and implementing sustainable reform." The discussions in both physical and virtual meeting spaces connect educators with real-world professionals, leaders in educational reform, and teacher leaders implementing new ideas. The vision of Create Something Great (2015) is to "provide opportunities for more integration across programs by linking educators and the community to discuss initiatives and programs." They accomplish this by

- empowering people to connect, take risks, share thinking, bring ideas, and take action;
- expanding thinking beyond the traditional practices in teaching and learning;
- providing opportunities for authentic dialogue to create, initiate, and implement a shift in instructional practice and learning environments; and
- bringing together a variety of voices and thinking.

This community of educators, who are learning together, is having a powerful impact on the transformation of education in their district. Encouraging leaders to organize this type of community is very actionable. It will produce strategies and plans to be implemented in classrooms that are aligned with new ideas in education and will impact personalized learning outcomes for students.

Assess What Matters Most in a Balanced Assessment System

Utilizing a Balanced Assessment System, all aspects of assessments—formative, interim, and summative—combine to help educators guide students on a personalized path of learning. Change the focus from standardized tests assessing a core curriculum, to assessing what matters most in the form of authentic assessments, narratives of learning, and actual products and services. Teachers should use individual or small group "target teaching" and make sure students know what they need in order to move forward with their interest-driven authentic assessments. This should replace the priority given to moving whole groups down the path of being successful on a standardized grade-specific test. Participate in state and national discussions promoting this thinking.

In Colorado's Douglas County School District, each school has a CITE 6 team. CITE is an acronym for Continuous Improvement of Teacher Effectiveness, and 6 refers to the designated standard where teachers are assessed based on student performance. Schools have the power to designate as a whole how specific assessments will impact teacher performance based on percentages. The district is pushing for larger percentages to be based on a student's body of evidence that would include authentic performance assessments. Smaller percentages would then be based on standardized test results. This action alone opens up the possibility for curriculum breadth and flexibility and helps to discourage current trends in which all students learn the same thing in the same way just to be successful on standardized tests and just in case they might need it in the future. To quote Dr. Elizabeth Fagen (2014), Superintendent of Douglas County Schools, "We hope to show that accountability in education can be done well, based on what is really important . . . we want to tie that (accountability) back to the most important things that our students should be learning for their lifetime, because that's the most important thing we do."

REFLECTION

Currently, teachers are being told what to teach and often how to teach in very prescribed manners, and teachers are accountable for high-stakes testing results. In many school districts, pay for performance is in place and if not now, in the near future, teacher salaries will be directly tied to student performance. Districts find themselves having to define and measure what matters most for their students as they set parameters for teacher accountability, and teachers are having to find creative ways to teach while at the same time making sure their students perform well on tests. As schools and districts look to offer more choices and options based on the expectations and needs of our students, they also cannot ignore the pressures of some parent communities that tie the success of their children to standards, test scores, and rote learning. "Our school is the best place for all kids, but it might not be the best place for all parents," states Mindy Persichina (personal communication, 2014), as she tours families through the halls of Lone Tree Elementary School, where she is the principal. She knows that the level of engagement is high and students are empowered to be leaders in real-world problem solving and to take ownership of their individual learning. The classrooms in her building look very different from traditional classrooms—flexible learning areas replace the idea of one desk for every student where it is typical to see all students working on the same task at the same time. Even though the students embrace this learning and this environment, some parents question it because it is different and they still believe that the way they learned is the only way to learn.

Balancing how we implement new ideas for educational reform and then present these new ideas to others who might expect a more traditional paradigm becomes the challenge.

Empowering our students to go beyond what we set for them, as a minimum, is an essential part of creating curriculum flexibility and breadth with personalization. As educators seek to deliver more impact in preparing students for their future, our task is to change the current approach of teaching students to follow in the footsteps of others by doing a good job of replicating someone else's work. Schools need to invent and implement new strategies, and create and curate resources, to engage students in real-world scenarios that lead to creative problem-solving, innovation, and the realization of their fresh ideas. Allowing students to take ownership of their learning within the confines of Common Core State Standards or national standards is only effective with a deeper understanding of the expected outcomes. Using the strategies discussed in this chapter will lead to personalized interest-driven inquiry that opens the doors for students to learn and retain substantially more than what the typical teacher-created curriculum may offer.

ACTIVITY #1: GLOBAL ISSUES CREATE OPPORTUNITIES FOR LEARNING

Participants

Teachers and students

Objective

Defined national standards are generally rooted in relevant real-world learning; however, to meet the needs of our subject-driven and age-separated school environments and testing requirements, they have been compartmentalized and pieced into small parts. Once these standards are "pulled apart," teachers in traditional models have worked to merge the standards into integrated units in order to create more meaning for students and to be more efficient in teaching all standards across a limited time frame. In this activity, participants will search for and analyze global issues that naturally integrate a pulled-apart standards-based curriculum. The purpose, however, is not to have teachers see how to plan a curriculum around real-world problems, but to see how it is possible for students to uncover more than required curriculum as they analyze and create solutions to real-world problems.

Materials

- Sticky notes and sheets of plain paper (8 ½ × 11)
- Internet access and digital tools for conducting web searches

Process

Have participants organize themselves in groups of two to four participants.

- Teachers: Organize groups according to the grade level they teach, and then subject area if applicable.
- Students: Organize groups according to interests or passions or goals.

What is the curriculum? (10 minutes)

- Teachers: Create a separate sticky note for the main areas of content they are required to cover across a year or term.
- Students: Create a separate sticky note for the outcomes for which they are creating a learning pathway.

What are the global issues? (15 minutes)

- Use digital tools to search lists of global issues
- Title sheets of paper with possible content-related global issues (three to four)

What is our challenge? Analyze which global issue would most effectively integrate the curriculum or list of desired outcomes. (15 minutes)

- For each issue, place sticky notes with any applicable content area or outcome on the titled sheet of paper.

- Total the number of sticky notes and write that number on the sheet of paper.
- Once one global issue is analyzed, move the sticky notes as needed to the next issue.

Share out: Share with the rest of the group the most pertinent global issues related to requirements of the Common Core State Standards.

ACTIVITY #2: INTENTIONALLY ALIGN STUDENT WORK TO STANDARDS

Participants

Teachers, school administrative teams, or district-level educators

Objective

The intentional alignment of personalized, student-driven learning to required content is what allows educators to not only connect standards to relevant learning pathways but to also include opportunities for expanded thinking that goes beyond standards. In this activity, participants will compare and contrast the two different approaches to this alignment as presented in this chapter.

Materials

- Personalized note-taking and idea generating tools

Organization: Groups of four to six participants.

Process

Individual review: Review the section in this chapter called "Intentionally Align Student Work to Standards." (10–15 minutes)

Two approaches and examples are given:

- Students as co-creators of their personalized curriculum
- Create a context for learning with a conceptual curriculum

Small group discussion: Compare and contrast these approaches/examples of how to align learning to standards. (10–15 minutes)

- How are these approaches similar and/or different?
- What is the value of using one approach as opposed to the other?
- Are there circumstances where one would work better than the other (i.e., younger vs. older learners)?

Individual application: Determine which approach would be doable for your specific circumstances and script a scenario for what this could look like for a small test-run using one of these approaches. (20 minutes)

Share out (15–20 minutes)

- Share your scenario with your small group.
- Decide which scenario will be shared with the larger group.
- Small groups share out one scenario to the larger group.

ACTIVITY #3: CREATE SYSTEMS FOR STUDENTS TO SELF-DOCUMENT INDIVIDUAL PROGRESS TOWARD STANDARDS

Participants

Teachers, school administrative teams, or district-level educators

Objective

Instead of assigning tasks and documenting student progress toward meeting a list of standards on a report card or progress report, consider putting systems in place for students to be in charge of this task. In this activity, participants will look at a couple strategies used at JCOS that empower students to create learning pathways, assess their own progress, and document their achievements.

- Analyze how a student outcomes inventory can be a tool to help implement this process.
- Create a prototype that could be used in their classroom, building, or district.

Materials

- Links to or copies of Jefferson County Open School Secondary Outcomes (https://drive.google.com/view erng/a/jeffcoschools.us/viewer?a=v&pid=sites&srcid= amVmZmNvc2Nob29scy51c3xqY29zfGd4OjNmZmI3 MzgzODQ5Zjc4MWE)
- Access to digital tools for document creation

Organization: Groups of four to six participants.

Process

Individual review: Review each strategy and evaluate how the strategies combine to impact student autonomy in personalized learning. (15 minutes)

1. JCOS Student Secondary Outcomes Inventory

2. Student-Created Transcripts at JCOS. Read this excerpt from the chapter:

   The culmination of each student's experience at the Open School is documented in the Final Transcript. Open School transcripts are written by the student and include a Personal Statement, class list, Advisor support letters, and a summary of each individual learning experience. Students include detailed information about knowledge and skills gained and what was of personal significance to the student. When a student includes an Open School class in his or her Transcript, this indicates that the student has met or exceeded all course requirements for that experience. Transcripts are authenticated by the student's academic Advisor, another faculty member familiar with the student's accomplishments, and the school Principal. The Transcript is the official record used for college and job applications.

Small group discussion: In small groups discuss the value and potential of using the following strategies. (10–15 minutes)

- In what ways do these strategies/tools empower students to script their own curriculum and take ownership of their learning?
- How could these strategies and tools be adapted for use across all grade levels?
- What value do these have for all stakeholders?

Individual application: Create a prototype for an effective tool or tools that will enable your students to self-document their progress toward a specific set of standards or outcomes. (20 minutes)

Partner review and feedback: Partner up to review and provide feedback. (20–30 minutes)

- Describe the challenge of your specific situation.
- Explain your prototype and steps to implement.
- Gather feedback.
- Answer questions as needed.
- Discuss strengths/weaknesses of idea.
- Consider suggestions.

REFERENCES

Bain, S. (2014). Jefferson County Open School, 2014–2015 Community "Owner's Manual." Retrieved April 24, 2015, from https://docs.google.com/a/jeffcoschools.us/viewer?a=v&pid=sites&srcid=amVmZmNvc2Nob29scy51c3xqY29zfGd4OjYwOTY3NDBjYzM3MDc3YTg

Barber, R. (2014, October 29). Teachers build Mosaic to empower kids. Retrieved April 24, 2015, from https://www.dcsdk12.org/teachers-build-mosaic-to-empower-students

bplearning. (2008, October 27). A Big Picture Learning student talks about the work at his LTI. Retrieved April 24, 2015, from https://www.youtube.com/watch?v=VXuWxmm9cmE

Create Something Great. (2015). Retrieved April 24, 2015, from https://sites.google.com/a/dcsdk12.org/create-something-great/about-csg-1

Create Something Great Google + Community. (2015). Retrieved April 24, 2015, from https://plus.google.com/communities/101899748631458053591

CV The Mosaic Collective. Retrieved July 8, 2015, http://www.cvmosaic.org/

Fagen, E. (2014). Douglas County strategic plan. Retrieved April 24, 2015, from https://www.dcsdk12.org/district/strategic-plan

Flick, L. (2014). Open education Philadelphia—The Workshop School. Retrieved April 24, 2015, from https://vimeo.com/81754232

International Center for Leadership in Education. (2015). Rigor/relevance framework. Retrieved April 24, 2015, from http://www.leadered.com/our-philosophy/rigor-relevance-framework.php

Jefferson County Open School. (2015). Retrieved April 24, 2015, from https://sites.google.com/a/jeffcoschools.us/jcos/student-homepage

Posner, R. (2009). *Lives of passion, school of hope: How one public school ignites a love of learning.* Boulder, CO: First Sentient Publications.

Reuter, J. (2014, June 27). Program expands definition of education. *Castle Rock News-Press.* Retrieved April 24, 2015, from http://castlerocknewspress.net/stories/Program-expands-definition-of-education,160861

Schneider, M. (2013, December 8). What is Mosaic? *The Collaboraider.* Retrieved April 24, 2015, from http://collaboraider.com/post/69395741424/what-is-mosaic

Workshop School. (2015). Mission statement. Retrieved April 24, 2015, from http://www.workshopschool.org

Zhao, Y. (2012). *World class learners: Educating creative and entrepreneurial students.* Thousand Oaks, CA: Corwin.

5

Mentoring and Guidance

The Role of Adults

by Homa Tavangar

... [W]e need adults to be passionate and talented in working with students as a community member. The more diverse their talents, the richer the intellectual environment is in the school.

(Zhao, World Class Learners, *2012, p. 180)*

Who's influenced you the most in your life?

My principal, Ms. Lopez.

How has she influenced you?

When we get in trouble, she doesn't suspend us. She calls us to her office and explains to us how society was built down around us. And she tells us that each time somebody fails out of school, a new jail cell gets built. And one time she made every student stand up, one at a time, and she told each one of us that we matter.

—Vidal, age 13, student at
Mott Hall Bridges
Academy (Stanton, January 20, 2015)

I want to be a real estate broker. My mentor is a real estate broker named Anthony Morris. He says that he can relate to what I'm going through because he grew up with a lot of challenges and had a hard time when he was younger.

How did you meet him?

One day I got in a fight with another girl in the hallway, and Principal Lopez said that she wouldn't suspend me if I spent a day with Mr. Morris.

—Female middle school student at
Mott Hall Bridges Academy
(Stanton, January 31, 2015)

Nadia (Lopez) is fearless. When she says that every kid can learn, she means it. And not only does she mean it, she puts systems in place to make it happen. It all begins with high expectations. When students arrive at this school, many of them are very behind. But Nadia sets high expectations on every one. She never says: "This student lives in the shelter so he deserves a break." or "Because of his parents, this student can't be expected to keep up." She says: "This is how we do things here, and there is no sidestepping."

—Mauriciere de Govia, Superintendent,
Brownsville School District
(Stanton, January 24, 2015)

Featured School

Mott Hall Bridges Academy, Brooklyn, New York

The three preceding quotations come from three different people describing Principal Nadia Lopez, of Mott Hall Bridges Academy, a public school in Brownsville, Brooklyn, the neighborhood with the highest crime rate in New York City, serving primarily children who live in nearby public housing projects. When Brandon Stanton took a photo and included the first quotation by Vidal in the caption for his wildly popular Humans of New York blog (http://www.humansofnewyork.com), an outpouring of support from around the world began: Within 5 days, readers had donated over $1 million to support the education of kids at Mott Hall Bridges Academy (Hu & Bromwich, 2015; Indiegogo Life, 2015; Rosenbaum, 2015), starting with funding a student trip to visit Harvard in order to raise students' expectations of what is possible for their own lives.

Besides the fact that Vidal's quote went viral, sparking an avalanche of goodness, followed by a series of short profiles from his school, the stories offer powerful lessons about the vital role of adults in spurring creative, student-driven, entrepreneurial learning, and ultimately, hope for a future that is very different from their present. As is evident from the quote above, Principal Nadia Lopez envisions that all of her students, regardless of their circumstances, meet the high expectations she sets. She has faith that all students can rise above their obstacles to achieve difficult goals. Most importantly, she ensures that systems are in place that will allow all students to achieve. As Principal Nadia Lopez demonstrates, the adults don't need to hold students' hands every step of the way, communities don't need to be financially well endowed, schools don't have to be perfect, and the lessons that stick rarely come from cramming for an exam. Rather, students are inspired when adults show through their daily actions (away from the spotlight) that they are willing to think outside the box for solutions to challenges great and small, that they believe in students' potential, that students matter, and that getting out into the world, tapping a range of expertise, yields important learning. For example, instead of suspending a student for

(Continued)

(Continued)

being involved in a fight, she instead offered her guidance and support—she gave the student an opportunity to meet with a mentor. And as is evident from the quote above, the student was then inspired to pursue a career she hadn't previously considered. She now has a goal for the future that she can work on, which she might not have had before meeting her mentor. In quote after quote from teachers and students at the school, we saw that Ms. Lopez didn't lower her standards for disadvantaged kids, but she helped them raise their sights so the students wanted to achieve greater results, using resources that went far beyond the building, staff, and textbooks provided by her school district.

As we see with Mott Hall Bridges Academy—and any school striving to offer its students world class learning—it truly "takes a village" and it includes adults possessing a range of skills and responsibilities who are alert to possibilities that can fill in gaps that will lead to meaningful 21st century learning, characterized by creativity, collaboration, diverse communication skills, and confronting increasingly complex material. In a student-driven learning environment, the role of adults isn't diminished; it just shifts. This chapter will look at that shift and how teachers can carve out effective roles to encourage and inspire creative, entrepreneurial learners who hope to impact the wider world.

STUDENT-DRIVEN LEARNING CREATES OPPORTUNITIES FOR ADULTS

In *World Class Learners,* Yong Zhao (2012) asserted that teachers will play many roles in the classroom, such as the

> "venture capitalist," who helps decide if the project is needed and feasible; the consultant, who provides suggestions and resources on demand; the motivator, who encourages at times of disappointment; the focus group, which provides feedback and critique on prototypes; and the partner, who provides complementary expertise and skills. (p. 203)

In Chapter 1 of this book, Zhao asserted, "Teachers become curators of learning opportunities and also 'tour guides' for students. They do not impose but can certainly mentor, motivate, and challenge."

Rather than feel potentially overwhelmed by these options, we consider the diverse roles of educators to present a great opportunity, a sort of liberation that helps feed the creative and service-oriented instincts that probably motivated teachers to venture into education in the first place. These diverse hats nonetheless represent a new paradigm for the teaching profession, and we realize it will take some time to develop the muscles, or skills and comfort level, called for by the various roles. Let's look at what some of these roles might entail.

Teacher as Venture Capitalist	Teacher as Partner
Teacher as Consultant	Teacher as Mentor
Teacher as Motivator	Teacher as Curator
Teacher as Focus Group	Teacher as Tour Guide

Teacher as Venture Capitalist

A venture capitalist is an investor who backs up a company (often a start-up) with funding and management expertise. In return, the venture capitalist can earn a massive return on his or her investments if these companies are a success. Hence, venture capitalists take an active, close-up interest in the success of their investments; evaluation is built into their process and as a condition for signing on as venture capitalists, they get to know their companies thoroughly. In order to learn and apply lessons from venture capitalists to education, we looked to a legendary venture capital firm, Sequoia Capital, which was an early investor in companies like Apple, Google, Cisco, Yahoo!, YouTube, Airbnb, and PayPal.

We highly encourage you to go directly to the Sequoia Capital website (http://www.sequoiacap.com). The values and vision conveyed can be inspiring for anyone looking to make a difference in any field. For example, to get a sense of the type of qualities they look for in their own team of venture capitalists, here's what Sequoia shares:

> The creative spirits. The underdogs. The resolute. The determined. The indefatigable. The defiant. The outsiders. The independent thinkers. The fighters. The true believers. . . . These are the kind of people we work with today.

This sounds a lot like a 21st century teacher of world class learners. If you apply this to your own teaching practice, it can help you pick up from a situation that seems like a failure, that is really stretching you (or your students), or that you might feel unprepared for—just as many entrepreneurs may feel. Wearing the hat of a venture capitalist, you take an active interest in your students—your active investments—and in return your students know that they need to push themselves to produce excellent products, as intelligently as possible. This is definitely a two-way relationship, and students can build their natural motivation when they know that you are investing in their genius, which they need to exert in order to raise the bar on the quality of all their work.

Teacher as Consultant

Unlike a traditional full-time worker, a consultant is available on demand: The company or entrepreneur's work takes place regardless, but with the realization that expertise from a consultant can enhance the quality, value, return on investment, or other key indicators of the enterprise. Teachers, acting as a consultant to student-driven learning, will be ready for their clients during times of particular need and serve as a trusted sounding board during key moments of development. Consultants may be aware of additional sources for conducting research, they may have already curated relevant materials to help advance a project, or they may know the right outside resource people to call on to keep advancing a work.

Teacher as Motivator

The role of teacher as motivator has been romanticized by many Hollywood movies, and it might be the reason many of us went into education in the first place. If only we could motivate students to reach their potential and achieve their personal best, the narrative often goes. The need for teacher as motivator goes far beyond a savior complex, since failure in entrepreneurial learning is inevitable. Not that we seek to fail, but in a creative, entrepreneurial environment, it's hard to imagine not falling down, then picking up and trying again. In positive terms, this is called "iteration." As the key adult in the classroom, showing students that iteration is valued and even expected serves as one of the most crucial, yet undervalued steps in a learning process.

To prepare students that even the smartest start-ups can fail, you can learn from the popular FailCon, or Failure Conference "for start-up founders to study their own and others' failures and prepare for success" (http://thefailcon.com). This experience of embracing and learning from failure is catching on among innovators globally: The conference has spread to over a dozen cities on six continents. If the brightest college graduates can fail and not hide it, can your students? This can serve as an important idea behind your role as motivator.

Teacher as Focus Group

Anyone with a good product or service idea knows that before hitting the market, they will need to test out all of the kinks with a focus group, usually an anonymous, objective, small sample of a population that might already be interested in the product or service. The focus group usually deliberates, almost as a jury would, on the product, service, or issue that is being presented to them and offers a fresh perspective that those who have been so close to the project can no longer offer.

This is a big responsibility for a single teacher, but the ability to step back and ask fresh, sincere questions to advance the success of the project serves as an invaluable development tool (and even a refreshing means for assessment). In addition, as we discuss later in this chapter, personalized learning means that you don't need to work alone to advance learning goals of your students: Tapping into the experience of diverse members of your wider community can enhance the focus group experience, as well as each of these roles for adults that we discuss in this section.

Teacher as Partner

There are times when, as the adult in class, you take on an authoritative (not authoritarian) role, and this may manifest itself in the venture capitalist or consultant role. At other times, students need a trusted partner, in whom to confide, who shares in the learning, and who can offer skills and expertise they didn't have themselves—in other words, a complementary role.

For example, a teacher who helped start a robotics club at her school had no prior expertise in robotics. She worked with students to learn the latest developments in the field, called on industry experts living within driving distance to coach them, and ultimately entered the group in a statewide competition. She didn't sponsor the club with a more developed expertise in robotics, but thanks to her connections, maturity, and professional position, she brought skills the students didn't have, while working alongside them to achieve an optimal outcome. The success achieved by club members at the state competition was everyone's success, and this created a sense of trust, friendship, and willingness to take intellectual risks on the part of the teacher as well as her students.

Teacher as Mentor

It is widely recognized that budding professionals, not just curious students, can advance farther and faster with good mentors in their lives. Teacher-mentors show by example a love of learning, creativity, and willingness to take intellectual risks and are an all-around example to their students. This may seem like a great deal of pressure to appear perfect, but it's much more about demonstrating care and consideration, while laying out a bigger vision of what is to come, what is at stake, and choices that might need to be made, based on your own experience. If as a teacher-mentor you can eliminate a culture of fear (fear of failure, fear of exams, fear of judgment) and instead create a positive culture (caring, encouraging, honest, nonjudgmental, iterative, supportive, respectful), this can surely unleash learning. Mentoring programs among at-risk youth have been shown to significantly positively impact student absenteeism, diminish drop-out rates, and improve recurring behavior problems (Herrera, DuBois, & Grossman, 2013). We believe that it's a healthy sign of growth that any student will inevitably struggle with social or academic issues as they progress through their education; having a trusted mentor can ease the vulnerability that students may feel.

Teacher as Curator

In Chapter 3, when discussing how teachers help cultivate student passions, the examples of Matt Cone in Carrboro, North Carolina, and Lou Lahana in New York City demonstrate the vital role of teachers as curators—using advanced knowledge to prepare high-quality information and resources on a range of topics relevant to class needs. Once information is curated, then it is up to the students to decide what to do with it. As Lou Lahana explained, this takes careful research and planning, but once he completes his curation, then his job becomes one of exposing students to a particular issue. This might take all of 3 minutes at the beginning of class; then students spend the rest of the time understanding the materials and issues for themselves and transforming this understanding into a "product" for an authentic audience.

Teacher as Tour Guide

If you've ever hired a tour guide when visiting somewhere new and notable, you may have experienced one of the following scenarios. In scenario A, you've met a guide who shared experiences, history, and hidden gems not found on standard written materials that you would have had difficulty finding on your own with any specific knowledge; one who knows the right amount of time you need to take in the view without feeling anxious or bored to move on; one who gives you space to explore without abandoning you; or one who you'd want to stay and have lunch with to continue learning about the wondrous place you are visiting. In scenario B, you've met a guide who seems to be reciting the Wikipedia page or the basic brochure summary that you knew before you got there; one who spends too much time (or not long enough) on each point; one who might be unclear in articulation; or one who might make you feel incompetent for not knowing enough, or make you bored because you weren't challenged or stimulated.

Anyone who's experienced scenario A knows what a tremendous difference a competent, encouraging, sensitive, respectful, empathetic tour guide can make. Teachers who demonstrate these same aptitudes can transform the learning experience in their class. They don't need to spoon-feed their students every fact or important point; rather, teachers guide them through well-curated pieces of information while also sharing their enthusiasm for the topic at hand. This serves as an important distinction, so professional educators doesn't feel like they are a babysitter or guide for aloof tourists.

PRINCIPLES FOR EXCELLENT MENTORING AND GUIDANCE

Expand Your Reach: Tap Into Resources Beyond the Classroom Walls

Because much as the new paradigm sees students as owners of their learning, instead of employees working to satisfy external standards delivered by lessons fed to them by adults working for the school, students are liberated to seek expertise from a wide variety of adults. For example, students can turn to those individuals quietly working behind the scenes to keep the school clean and cafeteria stocked, whose stories may rarely get heard, or global experts located thousands of miles away addressing public health or economic crises of entire nations.

The mere act of reaching out to individuals outside the classroom to contribute to student learning raises the bar of that learning: Students need to have a firmer grasp of the material before asking questions and probing outside resource people. An increasing number of schools are looking to outside experts to enhance STEM (science, technology, engineering, and mathematics) content or makerspaces. The example of tapping experts in Matt Cone's class at Carrboro High School demonstrates this: Students who had never before been trusted with honors-level material were calling on individuals like professors at Duke University, best-selling authors, or even the president of the World Bank to gain a deeper understanding of material and begin to address intractable social issues.

These early adapters show that despite the many roles teachers can opt to take, there are even more possibilities found when you tap into capable and willing resource people to support your students' learning. Principal Lopez in the Humans of New York example clearly did this, leveraging extremely limited material resources, channeling the uncontainable energy of one of her sixth graders to learn alongside a local real estate broker. As we see throughout examples sprinkled in this three-book series, many other teachers have sought global issue experts, teachers in schools on the other side of the world, and parent volunteers, among others, to enhance student-driven learning. Here are some examples of who and how to tap into to benefit students.

As you start to consider outside lecturers, mentors, cheerleaders, and subject area experts, you can consider inviting anyone within driving distance (and beyond, as we discuss later in this chapter) to encourage your students' personalized learning. Here is just a sample of the sort of people you might call on to collaborate with your students and you:

Possible (In-Person) Resource People to Call On for Your Students:

- Local professionals like computer programmers, physicians, nurses, hospital administrators, research scientists, engineers, social media experts, veterinarians, accountants, financial planners, business executives, managers, contractors, graphic designers, architects, government employees, journalists, and chefs
- Tradespeople like electricians, plumbers, and carpenters
- Retired professionals
- Exchange students and international/foreign university students
- University professors
- Executives in nonprofit organizations locally or globally
- Authors of any genre
- Local- and state-level political representatives, organizers, and lobbyists
- Country experts (can draw from any of the people listed above with experience living in a particular country of interest, families of students, or other school staff)
- Specialized networks, like returning Peace Corps volunteers, rotary clubs and other local organizations with a global and service focus, professional groups, and members of interfaith organizations

Nonprofit organization One To World's Global Classroom (http://www.one-to-world.org) connects New York City youth with trained, international university scholars through in-person, interactive workshops that engage students in learning about world cultures and global issues. Interaction with Global Guides offers students a platform to break down stereotypes and expand their perspectives, and it can serve as a model for bringing in outside experts to work with students in a school, even if One To World's services can't reach your school directly.

Local media outlets provide another possible source of great resources for your class. Be on the lookout for stories that profile the work of people doing interesting things in your area, and encourage your students to do the same.

Take Advantage of Visitors Coming to Your School or Community for Meaningful Interaction

EduCon, an education conference focusing on innovation and the future of schools, is organized annually by staff and students at Science Leadership Academy (SLA) in Philadelphia, a school we've discussed throughout this book. One thing that makes EduCon stand out is the fact that the SLA students themselves are involved in setting up and running the respected conference, alongside their teachers and administrators. This goes way beyond hooking up computers for presentations and sprucing up classrooms; students join the front lines of the national conversation on the future of education, and make presentations themselves. This serves as a source of pride for the students, as well as another component that distinguishes the inquiry-driven school. Describing their ultimate motivation for the monumental effort of putting on EduCon in the midst of the school year, Principal Chris Lehmann (2015) shares:

> And that's why we do it. Because our kids look at all of you who have come to learn with and from them and they realize that they really can help to change the world. EduCon is that moment for many of our students when they prove to themselves that they can be active, authentic agents in the world beyond their school.

> As powerful as the learning all the educators will do over the next three days can be, for me, that lesson may be the powerful thing that any of us learn all weekend.

Can you think of other ways that you might help facilitate student interactions with visitors or experts coming to your school, district, or community? How about setting up Question & Answer sessions with teacher trainers, certification teams, or consultants working with administrators? What about inviting building engineers or environmental or food inspectors to come talk to your class about their work and specific issues that challenge them? You don't need to organize an elaborate event to benefit from visitors who might really enjoy speaking with your students.

Take Advantage of Virtual Partners and Mentors

Just as technology and information resources work together to help open doors for a global classroom, calling on global mentors and partners for your students (or for your own learning or collaboration efforts in building your teaching practice) can be facilitated by virtual—yet authentic—connections with people located way beyond driving distance.

Some examples of virtual partners and mentors might include the following:

- Skype an author—then go beyond the initial video chat with the author. If some students were particularly enthusiastic about the author's work or the conversation, encourage them to continue the relationship. Offer some prompts for follow-up, whether it is to pursue deeper research, expand creative writing capability, or simply prepare for a follow-up conversation. The beauty of this platform is that it works for a variety of authors, from picture book and young-adult fiction authors to researchers with prominent publications in genomic testing or climate change. If it is difficult to maintain follow-up Skype sessions, students can maintain contact via Twitter, Facebook, e-mail, or other platforms of the author's choosing.
- Build your own professional learning network (PLN)— with members located anywhere in the world, communicating via social media or a specialized Ning, or brought together via comments in a blog. A PLN can connect you with other like-minded educators interested

in innovation in the classroom and extend to collaborating on building a specific lesson together, or sharing a challenge and helping each other overcome it. Members of your PLN might even be interested in conducting a teaching exchange with a class: If they have a topic they are passionate about teaching, they could launch the lesson to your class via a video call, or join in to pose some of their own driving questions. This also helps your students gain a wider appreciation for your work and their own, and this demonstrates that you also are continuously learning and expanding your professional skills.

- Hacktivism. Hashtag activism has been criticized as armchair activism or too superficial. The claim is that sharing a tweet of just 140 characters does not constitute an invested engagement. This might be true, yet we've also seen repeatedly how engaging in an important global issue via social media can connect young people to those closest to the event or issue as it is unfolding. A few tweets and a conversation that can begin from there suddenly turns the learner into one who has become invested in the matter, whether it's #StuVoice (student voice movement), #BlackLivesMatter, or #JeSuisCharlie. As an example of adult/teacher guidance in social media activism and engagement, help your students distinguish between authentic, growth-oriented engagement versus postings that try to gain the most attention (as in online shaming and bullying, or following celebrity sightings).

Guiding Student-Driven Learning: Less of a GPS and More of an Art Class

With so many options in terms of the roles teachers can play and the fascinating people to call on to enhance student experience, what does the day-to-day teacher experience look like where the student learning is creative, personalized, and product oriented?

As we imagined the best metaphor for the role of adults in this new paradigm of learning, we thought it looks less like a GPS that gives step-by-step guidance and more like a good art teacher who:

- Gives parameters for what is expected,
- Offers a vision of real skills you'll need,
- Points you in the direction of learning the history of what you'll be working on, and
- Lets passion and creativity drive you.

With this grounded yet creative ideal in mind, the following are some tips for the role of adults in encouraging personalized learning.

If You're Just Beginning

- Consider the hats you'd like to wear—such as a coach, partner, venture capitalist, or curator—or come up with your own original role. Activity 2 at the end of this chapter can help you more clearly visualize your role in these various positions.
- Adjust the language of your feedback to students. For example, students benefit from honest critique along with positive attention for their projects. Constant praise can be a hindrance. While helping them weigh various sides, saying something like "Have you considered this?" or "You might want to look at that." can advance them forward in their learning.
- Recognize that there is not one right answer, argument, position, or issue that you're looking for students to present in a narrow way. This can get uncomfortable; be okay with that. Make sure students understand this point.
- Establish a culture of respect, empathy, and open communication. This includes seeing failure as part of an iterative process, not something to be ashamed of; encouragement and adult or peer support for those who

are struggling; and setting a standard of not judging brainstorming or comments during discussion, no matter how out there an idea may be.

- As part of the changed culture, make it clear that your classroom's focus is on students (learners), not the teacher. This can be reflected in changing the room layout to be student centered, practicing more active listening, and letting go of feeling like you need to personally explain all of the information in a unit.

- Specify expectations—for students and adults. Even for visiting adults, knowing what is expected of them, as well as what isn't, will help produce a positive, two-way relationship.

- Spend time considering driving questions you will have students work on and explore. The best questions will leave students with plenty of work to do, guided by their interests and strengths. They will also allow the teacher to get out of the way, so students can really dive into learning challenging material.

- Break down specific learning units by creating a timeline with milestones. This allows students to have built-in accountability, even while personalizing their learning and the products that demonstrate their learning. Such milestones include relevant deadlines, time for peer review, time to consider (and compose) big and small topical questions, class time to work on the project, and periodic reflection and self-evaluation before the final product is submitted.

If You've Got Some Experience

- All of the above points will call for revisiting and continuous improvement, so these remain important whatever your experience level.

- Each marking period, check back on your milestones and progress toward enhancing the participatory culture in your class to reflect on any changes, progress, or challenges.

- When inviting adults from the community to work with your students, coach them on useful language, particularly because you will know your students better. For example, go over the principles you used in the early stages of coaching, such as resisting offering constant praise, and instead giving honest, gentle feedback, interacting respectfully as you would with a peer and not talking down to the learner.
- As you let go of your traditional teacher role at the front of the classroom, offer opportunities for other adult or student collaborators to lead a class.
- Flip your classroom and have students return to class ready to teach their topic creatively.
- Call upon other teachers in your building or district to collaborate in considering new resource people to bring in to work with students or in reconsidering their role in the class with you.
- Share your experience with your PLN.

If You're Ready to Adapt This on a Wider Scale or Are More Experienced

- Share your experience with wider networks so that others may learn and share their thoughts with you. You might start off by tweeting your experiences with your PLN; as your voice and experience develop, consider starting a blog, even if you are your only audience. The blog serves as a longer-form platform for thoughtful reflection and self-assessment.
- Recommend sharing your experience of reconsidering adults' roles in your class for schoolwide or districtwide inservice training, so that colleagues can replicate the new paradigm with their own students. Be honest about successes and failures. Sugar-coating hiccups won't benefit anyone.
- Create shared plans with colleagues in your district. Take advantage of diverse strengths and interests to co-create better learning experiences.

- Considering raising resources but look beyond traditional funding sources to advance your goals. Encourage student fundraising, crowdfunding (e.g., through sites like gofundme.com, kickstarter.com, or donorschoose. org) or stay in touch with foundations, arts organizations, nonprofits, corporations, service clubs, and your home and school association (or parent teacher organization) to help fund individual or group field trips, bring in visiting artists or an artist in residence, and purchase supplies or subscriptions for research. The fundraising effort can seem overwhelming amid many other demands, so this is a great job to outsource to a parent or other volunteer.

Overcoming Challenges

If I take on various hats for students to learn on their own or encourage them to work with outside mentors, will this impact my ability to guide students to learn as much as they can?

If I get out of the way for students to learn on their own, then my job security will diminish. Will teachers start to be unnecessary?

What if students develop a closer relationship with outside mentors and guides than with me, their teacher? Will this make my work irrelevant?

If adults working with students aren't aware of testing requirements and pedagogy, won't my students bomb the tests? This also will reflect badly on my teaching.

These reflect some of the natural concerns that are expressed when we encourage a new role for adults. Early, anecdotal experience demonstrates over and over again that when teachers roll out the initiatives encouraged here at a pace they are comfortable with, the results are overwhelmingly positive: Student motivation soars, resulting in better test results, and more importantly, growing passion, drive, self-worth, and curiosity to keep learning. If anything, trying this new, entrepreneurial role for adults can benefit your teaching practice (and job satisfaction) tremendously.

REFLECTION

Opening up a classroom to a new model of adult mentoring and guidance can expose teachers to a whole new level of vulnerability—as well as fulfillment and promise. The traditional school experience of standing in front of a classroom offering the information that would appear on an assessment at the end of a unit essentially progresses along a straight line, going from point A to point B. This new model proposes something messier and more creative. Seeing yourself as a curator, investor, or partner calls for the exercise of new skills and introduces more surprises to the learning process. You are becoming an entrepreneurial teacher: alert to possibilities, and open to change and growth to benefit your practice. This particularly becomes apparent when other adults are invited to lead a class, mentor a project, or consult on the outcome of product-oriented learning. The sheer presence of diversity of personalities, experience, and culture complicates the learning. At the same time, the same diversity enriches learning immensely and can help produce a whole new learning experience that no traditional classroom experience could ever hope to replicate. We hope this is a risk that you will consider worth taking. Introducing diverse adult roles becomes more doable amid a gradual rollout, as we have seen across ideas throughout this book. As you consider new roles for yourself and other adults coming to your class, ask yourself the following questions:

- What stumbling blocks do my students repeatedly experience?
- If I took on a role of consultant, curator, venture capitalist, or tour guide, could the new approach help advance

inquiry and mastery? Can the new roles address my student stumbling blocks in a fresh light?

- How could an outside expert or encourager help advance or turn around the learning environment in my classroom?
- Which relationships or experiences would be beneficial for my students: locals coming in to the class, students going out to experience various work environments, group field trips, or virtual conversations with peers or adults farther away?
- Are there other colleagues in the building who would be interested in trying new roles in their own classroom and/or bringing in other adults to lend their support to the class? This way, you can try new hats with the benefit of a compassionate, encouraging sounding board.

ACTIVITY #1: HOW WILL YOU USE THOSE RESOURCE PEOPLE?

Participants

Teachers

Objective

This chapter introduced various ways to bring on diverse individuals to enhance your students' experience in your class. This activity sets aside time to plan, consider, invite, and share a plan for bringing in outside adults to work with your students.

Materials

The following materials are needed:

- Tablet or laptop computer (Internet-enabled), with e-mail

Process

(60 minutes)

- Brainstorm at least three specific individuals you might call on to enhance your student's learning experience. If three relevant individuals don't come to mind within a few minutes, start researching local media outlets (e.g., public radio stations, local newspapers, or local social media channels) to gather some names of interesting/ potentially helpful people.
- What would you like to ask them to do with your students?
- Create an action plan for partnering with three people in the coming school year.
- Write your first e-mail inviting the first guest to your class or to work with a specific student.
- Share and reflect with the group: Who are you going to call on? How will they (ideally) help your students? What concerns do you have about outreach?

Note: Most schools and districts have a background check policy in place for all adults who will interact with students, in order to protect student safety. Make sure you know and comply with your school policy. If your school doesn't have a policy in place, consider having adults who will have one-on-one contact with students sign a waiver. Talk to your school's legal office to make sure you have this background step in place prior to implementing this approach.

ACTIVITY #2: SO MANY HATS!

Participants

Teachers.

Objective

Just as in Activity 1 above, this activity sets aside time to organize, consider, and share a plan—yet instead of looking to outside resources, this activity asks you to look inward and draw from your own talents and interests.

Materials

The following materials are needed:

- Tablet or laptop computer (Internet-enabled), with e-mail

Process

- In this chapter, we described the many roles of a teacher where student-driven learning prevails. List all of the hats you wear throughout your day, from the time you wake up until you go to sleep. Can you leverage some of your roles to enhance the quality of learning in your classroom? Are you adequately drawing on your talents, interests, and skills?
- Create a list of all your roles from the highest priority to the lowest. Are there some roles you might be able to eliminate or streamline so you don't feel so stretched?
- Among the roles listed in this chapter, are there some that you would like to take on with your students? List some action steps that you can take to more fully assume a new role in your class.
- Consider colleagues whose teaching practice you admire. What are some of the hats they are wearing to enhance their students' learning experience?
- Share and reflect on roles you think you are doing well and which ones you'd like to improve.

REFERENCES

EduCon. (2015, January). Power to the people: Distributed leadership as a pathway to change. Retrieved February 1, 2015, from http://2015.educon.org/conversations/power_to_the_people-distributed_leadership_as_a_pathway_to_change

FailCon. Retrieved April 24, 2015, from http://thefailcon.com

Herrera, C., DuBois, D. L., & Grossman, J. B. (2013). *The role of risk: Mentoring experiences and outcomes for youth with varying risk profiles*. New York, NY: A Public/Private Ventures project distributed by MDRC. Retrieved February 5, 2015, from http://www.mdrc.org/sites/default/files/Role%20of%20Risk_Final-web%20PDF.pdf

Hu, W., & Bromwich, J. (2015, January 29). A boy praises the principal of his Brooklyn school, and a fund-raising campaign takes off. *New York Times*. Retrieved February 6, 2015, from http://www.nytimes.com/2015/02/01/nyregion/a-boy-praises-the-principal-of-his-brooklyn-school-and-a-fund-raising-campaign-takes-off.html?_r=1

Indiegogo Life. (2015). Let's send kids to Harvard: Vidal Scholarship Fund. Retrieved April 28, 2015, from https://life.indiegogo.com/fundraisers/let-s-send-kids-to-harvard

Lehmann, C. (2015, January 23). The night before. Retrieved February 5, 2015, from http://practicaltheory.org/blog/2015/01/23/the-night-before/

One To World. (2015). Who we are. Retrieved March 1, 2015, from http://www.one-to-world.org

Rosenbaum, S. (2015, February 2). 'Humans of New York' blogger raises over $1M for students. *New York Post*. Retrieved February 6, 2015, from http://nypost.com/2015/02/02/humans-of-new-york-blogger-raises-over-1m-for-students/

Sequoia. (2015). Culture. Retrieved April 24, 2015, http://www.sequoiacap.com/us/about/dentmakers

Stanton, B. (2015, January 20). Humans of New York. Retrieved March 3, 2015, from http://www.humansofnewyork.com/post/108621363306/whos-influenced-you-the-most-in-your-life-my

Stanton, B. (2015, January 24). Humans of New York. Retrieved March 3, 2015, from http://www.humansofnewyork.com/post/109012552401/i-only-had-a-few-minutes-to-speak-with-ms-lopez

Stanton, B. (2015, January 31). Humans of New York. Retrieved March 3, 2015, from http://www.humansofnewyork.com/post/109710810381/i-want-to-be-a-real-estate-broker-my-mentor-is-a

Zhao, Y. (2012). *World class learners: Educating creative and entrepreneurial students*. Thousand Oaks, CA: Corwin.

6

Flexible Spaces, Schedules, and Roles

Enabling Personalization

by Kay Tucker

> Let's hope that scientific evidence . . . will set us on a new path—one in which we break down the . . . walls that keep our children trapped in boxes. . . We first need to free ourselves from the mental box that limits our thinking about the real meaning and purpose of education.
>
> *Prakash Nair (2011)*

A flexible environment allows and enables personalization. Children should have the freedom to self-select when and how to make use of available resources. [. . .]But freedom is not sufficient; there should be an infrastructure designed to assist children to personalize their learning experiences, because children may not be aware of or understand what is available and how they may be meaningful.

(Zhao, World Class Learners, *2012, p. 181)*

Featured School

Monument Mountain Regional High School, Great Barrington, Massachusetts

"It is crazy that in a system that is meant to teach and help the youth, there is no voice from the youth at all." This statement begins a video by Charles Tsai (2013) titled "If Students Designed Their Own Schools. . . ." The video brings to life The Independent Project, in which students created and implemented a semester of studies at Monument Mountain Regional High School. Tests and quizzes were eliminated and students designed their own learning material and taught each other. They removed the idea of classes and most of the time they did not include teachers or adults in the room. Students posed their own questions and independently found the answers as they removed the role of teachers as direct instructors.

The Independent Project is a school within a public high school—an alternative academic program. The students focus on the core areas of English, math, social sciences, and natural sciences, and they apply the basic rule of designing their own learning. On Mondays, the students each come up with a question related to one of the core subjects. On Fridays, after spending the week researching and experimenting, they present what they have learned to the other students. "The most important thing about your question is that you actually want to know the answer. . . . If the question is yours, the answer actually feels great when you obtain it" (Tsai, 2013). This comment from the video affirms how this component of the school design succeeds in increasing the level of student engagement, and it also explains why students want their presentations to be as engaging as possible.

Weekly questions make up about half of the students' time and the other half is spent on "individual endeavors." These are challenging tasks that span the entire term and must demonstrate effort, learning, and mastery of a skill. The examples given in the video are varied: learn to play an instrument, write a novel, research topics such as education or the environment, and create a "mockumentary" of the school. Participating in discussions among peers and having the time to grow and change a passion-driven project in an open-ended manner are ideas that are valued by the students. For this pilot, the team of students designated the last 3 weeks of the semester to be spent on a "collective endeavor." This collaborative time was designed with the specific aim of students working together to make a difference and produce social impact while engaging in a learning experience at the same time.

Marianne Young, principal of this public high school in Massachusetts, took a risk by giving credence to an innovative idea presented to her by a student—to allow students to create their own learning environment that was more engaging and led to greater mastery than was being offered in teacher-designed classes. Her openness to this idea and the fact that it came to fruition stem from her belief that: "My personal and professional investment into these opportunities is to create a school and a way of educating young people that allows it to be completely invested. And to stop trying to move every kind of human being through the same gate" (Tsai, 2013, 5:47–6:13).

This example shows how empowering students to take charge of their learning and to be autonomous learners naturally forced a change in how education currently functions. These students broke apart the following paradigms of classrooms as defined spaces, classes as blocks of time specified to learn a specific subject, and teachers as the ones in charge of student learning. In changing up these paradigms, the students accomplished what they set out to do: They created an environment for learning that was engaging and allowed them to reach mastery in the subject areas about which they were passionate. They learned and taught others about things they cared about, they dedicated time to follow their passions, and they collaboratively impacted social change.

PRINCIPLES BEHIND PERSONALIZATION WITH FLEXIBLE SPACES, SCHEDULES, AND ROLES

The same principles that clarify the effectiveness of the Monument Mountain Regional High School example are also behind the following Wooranna Park Primary School (WPPS) example.

Students Dictate the *Where,* *When,* and *How* of Learning

(See Activity #1: When, Where, and How Depends on What)

"Children come to school with a self-directed purpose, an openness to possibilities and an eagerness to work collaboratively with their classmates" (Perlman, 2012). Setting the stage for this type of learning, WPPS in Victoria, Australia, reversed traditional models in which teachers require things of students, to a new approach where students require the skills, knowledge, and guidance of their teachers. Learning is personalized and differentiated, and it is based on an authentic and real-world approach. At WPPS, large groups of students work with many teachers in a single environment—this is very different from traditional classrooms, in which one teacher is mainly responsible for a group of approximately 20–30 students in a contained classroom. To meet this challenge, WPPS realized they needed to create a learning environment that included flexible spaces, flexible schedules, and even flexible roles for teachers.

The video "Tomorrow's School Today" captures the essence of how WPPS combines a physical environment that facilitates student learning with new approaches to teaching and learning. The narrator explains:

> After meeting with their home-group teacher, children move to various experiences determined according to their individual learning journey. Teachers, working collaboratively throughout the day, take on various roles to support the children in negotiating individual learning goals. (Perlman, 2012)

The following list of typical scenarios at WPPS illustrates how teachers and students work together in this flexible environment:

- One-on-one conference times to guide and support students in setting learning goals

- Target teaching with small group instruction responding to individual needs
- Workshops as a means of provoking thinking for project work
- Learning agreement time when students are free to schedule their independent or collaborative work on projects, or respond to their provocations in the physical environment

Students arrange their entire schedule as they plan what they need to accomplish in a week. Their projects may take only a couple of weeks, or they may span the entire school year. Workshops are offered multiple times, giving students choice as to when they feel it is best to attend in order to help them reach their goals.

Where We Learn Matters

At WPPS, there is also a focus on creating stimulating environments as a means of setting the stage for personalized interest-driven inquiry. With younger students, they have found an exciting way to conceptualize learning and trigger the discovery of new knowledge through creative problem solving. Teachers provoke thinking by asking questions and immersing the students in stimulating learning platforms (SLPs). SLPs are physical areas that tap into a child's imagination, are interdisciplinary, and are highly experiential. Dragon Boat and Spaceship are environments specifically created to inspire students in Year 2 and Year 3 learning units. SLPs are designed to encourage creative play within a context for learning. The Enigma Portal for older students is based on David Thornburg's (2014) idea of a holodeck, as presented in *From the Campfire to the Holodeck: Creating Engaging and Powerful 21st Century Learning Environments*. Holodecks are rooms he refers to as "theaters without audiences." The idea of no audience equates to a room full of actors, with everyone on the same par. This eliminates any sense of what he calls "full frontal" or "spray and pray" teaching as direct instruction (Thornburg, 2007).

All of these interactive experiences make up a rich and diverse physical environment that sparks student interest and curiosity and begins the valuable questioning process that leads to self-directed purposeful learning.

Flexible Spaces, Schedules, and Roles Combine to Transform Learning

(See Activity #2: ST-RE-T-CH It Out!)

Spaces and schedules in schools have changed very little since the 1950s—yet almost everything else is in our current world is very different. What is sometimes referred to as a "cells and bells" philosophy is what most of our schools are designed to accommodate. Prakash Nair, one of the leading change agents in school design, advocates for the fact that our places of teaching and learning need to align with 21st century learning goals. In one of his commentaries in *Education Week*, entitled "The Classroom Is Obsolete: It's Time for Something New," Nair (2011) sets forth a key set of principles for design: (1) personalized, (2) safe and secure, (3) inquiry based, (4) student directed, (5) collaborative, (6) interdisciplinary, (7) rigorous and hands-on, (8) embodying a culture of excellence and high expectations, (9) environmentally conscious, (10) offering strong connections to the local community and business, (11) globally networked, and (12) setting the stage for lifelong learning.

These principles for design are evident in both The Independent Project and the WPPS examples we've described. The overriding idea of flexibility creates a fluid learning environment, one that adapts to all of the variables associated with groups of diverse learners consistent with Nair's key principles. As the focus of education shifts away from teaching to learning, teachers need to adapt their practices and become co-learners and facilitators of learning in a student-directed environment. Opening up to the idea of change and flexibility in our roles should be a standard for personalized learning. Empowering students to drive their own flexible options for how, when, and where they learn allows for powerful change.

WPPS is a proven example of how to personalize learning using the power of flexibility across several areas related to learning and teaching. In an article titled "What Would a School Built by Walt Disney Look Like?," Principal Ray Trotter explains why WPPS transformed their learning environments and teaching practices. "Traditionally schools, despite their core purpose, have been places built to service the needs of teachers, rather than learners. They are places where we 'pour' knowledge into students, rather than excite their appetite for learning and where their achievements are graded and compared, rather than celebrated" (Trotter, 2015). Australia's Building the Education Revolution program recently committed a large amount of money to upgrading schools, but Trotter contends that changes in buildings alone will not lead to the needed reform in teaching practice and that this problem is twofold. "Many teachers believe that the traditional one teacher classroom is still the best way to educate students and, sadly, many teachers simply don't understand why or how to teach in the more contemporary learning environments" (Trotter, 2015).

WPPS sets this as their mission: to provide students with a learning environment that recognizes children learn best when engaged with real-world, authentic tasks, involving problem solving and collaboration with peers on interdisciplinary, research-based project work; where the teacher's role includes that of coach and facilitator, and where students are empowered to take responsibility for their learning. WPPS purposefully developed an inclusive framework to support this mission, one they refer to as their raison d'être or reason for being. The physical design at WPPS is targeted in their raison d'être as being able to support comfortable, aesthetically pleasing learning environments. Intentionally designing diverse spaces that are always available to students and teachers enables them to facilitate learning as they move from one setting to another throughout the day. Their pedagogy was the driving force behind the creation of their flexible spaces, schedules, and roles, but now this interdependent quality is what creates a sustainable environment for teaching and learning.

FLEXIBLE SPACES, SCHEDULES, AND ROLES ARE PART OF AN EDUCATIONAL ECOSYSTEM THAT WORKS

(See Activity #3: Create an Ecosystem for Learning)

Modern schools need to look beyond their four walls, their set schedules, and the roles their teachers play and create what is called a learning ecosystem. This ecosystem combines physical and virtual spaces to create formal and informal learning opportunities on a 24/7 basis. It includes environments and practices that are most conducive in engaging students in the activities needed to acquire relevant skills and knowledge. A white paper titled, "Developing an Innovation Ecosystem for Learning," written by Valerie Hannon, Alec Patton, and Julie Temperley of Cisco, addresses the idea of engaging with learning and not just engaging in school. It implies that with the current pressures and opportunities in the world, people need to acquire multiple forms of literacy (e.g., cross-cultural, ecological, etc.). This enables people of all ages to:

> ... be lifelong learners, because technology, politics, economics, and the environment are changing so quickly. This demands a shift away from focusing on engagement in school, to engagement in learning. It also requires an examination of what sorts of environments are most conducive to learning in (and for) the 21st Century. (Hannon, Patton, & Temperley, 2011)

The impact of emerging innovative technologies that support different modes of learning has changed the way we think about education—it has broadened our opportunities for collaboration and given us easy access to unlimited continuous information. In shifting the focus from going to school to learn to engaging students in learning, these ecosystems should be flexible and interconnected and promote learner ownership. This is the realm that fosters the connections between formal and informal learning because it occurs within and outside of the classroom. It should also be the impetus for teachers to take advantage of all opportunities for learning as they shift their role away from delivering content to facilitating learning that happens beyond the classroom walls.

Alicia Pepe, a sixth-grade teacher at Lone Tree Elementary in Colorado, had her students create designs for the "perfect" classroom. She offered them the freedom to rid the room of desks and start from scratch. These students now spend their days learning in an environment that looks nothing like a typical classroom. Areas in her classroom include couch-like comfortable seating areas, options for gathering around circular tables either standing or sitting on short upholstered stools, a maker-table surrounded with stools set among baskets of available material, a place for mobile digital tools (iPads, MacBooks, Chromebooks) available to use in any of the spaces, large-screen iMacs in separate areas for individual or small group Hangouts or Skype sessions, a presentation area, and a "campfire" area. Three Spheros, app-controlled balls, sit on the shelf as class pets. Students play games or write code on iPads to move these robotic pets around the room. The class captures both how they are engaged in learning and what they are learning, and students use both Twitter and Instagram to disseminate information. They use social media as a tool to expand their horizons and to create global connections. All students have access to Google Apps for Education and they have websites as e-portfolios. Personalized homework takes the form of online math forums, flipped classroom options, and research for project work. Pepe does not have a defined schedule for content delivery, but she instead designates large blocks of time for students to work on their projects and individual goals as she conferences and mentors to meet individual needs. All of the learning applies to the creation of authentic assessments with no set due dates as students develop and grow their ideas for real-world application across the entire year. They set personal schedules with ample time for product development involving feedback and revisions. Pepe has purposefully aligned her physical and virtual spaces to create an ecosystem for learning that is collaborative and rich with resources and leads to personalized learning.

Learning Based on Projects and Passions, Not Subjects

Unlike traditional high schools, classes at The Workshop School in Philadelphia, Pennsylvania, are not divided by subject. Instead they are divided by project—interdisciplinary inquiry-based projects where students are solving real-world problems. In the following, Simon Hauger talks about student schedules at The Workshop School:

> Two-thirds of the day they have project blocks and the academics are integrated into the blocks. Seminars are content focused, but when they work well, they actually inform the projects. . . we need to get rid of false academic distinctions. No one in real life says it's 8:54—now I'm doing Social Studies. . . it's now 9:34—I am becoming a scientist." (Flick, 2014)

The Workshop School's Lighting 52nd Street project speaks to success with this approach.

> This spring, a group of students completed a project focused on electricity. They learned how electricity is generated and how different kinds of circuits work. They wired lamps, built a bike generator, and created a solar charging system. Working with the Enterprise Center, a West Philadelphia minority business incubator, students analyzed lighting needs along the 52nd Street business corridor, a major commercial thoroughfare in West Philadelphia. Then they designed and built two different energy efficient lighting prototypes and

presented their designs to the Enterprise Center, the City Councilwoman Jannie Blackwell, a local Community Development Corporation, and representatives of the Philadelphia Department of Commerce. In the next phase of the project, students will develop a business and production plan, building on previous work and community feedback. (Workshop School, 2015)

The success of these examples stems from the fact that learning was driven by real-world projects or passions, and the integrated approach to learning was natural. Learning based on this approach makes sense to learners—they are doing work that matters to them, as opposed to learning segments of content that might apply to the bigger, more relevant picture.

STRATEGIES AND IDEAS FOR PERSONALIZED LEARNING WITHIN FLEXIBLE ENVIRONMENTS

In the Classroom

Create a Flexible Environment in Your Classroom

Engage students in creating a design for your classroom that addresses how they learn best and enables them to move to various areas. Consider how to move the focus of learning. If you have a "frontal focus" due to a white board/projector combo, think about how to spread out more individualized or small group learning. A great place to start is to assign areas of the room according to Thornburg's work. Where will you locate your watering hole(s)? Is there an area to create an appealing campfire? How are digital tools being used to create these virtual environments?

Combine Flexible Physical and Virtual Spaces

All of the examples in this chapter combine current digital tools with an innovative environment. Similar to how Alicia

Pepe combined physical spaces with virtual spaces to achieve a total environment, think about how these two weave together to impact learning.

- Do you have tools available for your students, such as Google Apps for Education?
- Are you using Google Classroom to manage student learning?
- Are students accessing 24/7 learning opportunities that can happen outside of school and without a teacher?
- Do your students have access to tools and resources to help them collaborate?

In "The Classroom Is Obsolete: It's Time for Something New," Prakash Nair (2011) emphasizes how students learn:

Each student 'constructs' knowledge based on his or her own past experiences. Because of this, the research demands a personalized education model to maximize individual student achievement. Classrooms, on the other hand, are based on the erroneous assumption that efficient delivery of content is the same as effective learning.

With this in mind, consider the effectiveness of merging the digital world with the physical world as a means of moving past efficient delivery of content to opportunities for your students to construct their own learning.

Transform Teaching and Learning With a Flexible Ecosystem

A flexible learning ecosystem reflects a transformation of teaching. "Getting rid of my teacher desk/table forces me to meet with all of the students, instead of them always coming to me," comments Alicia Pepe (2015). She goes on to explain how students have taken ownership of their environment, how they suggest moving things around, and how they set up for learning. When a Lego robotics kit unexpectedly arrived in the classroom (donated by someone on DonorsChoose.org), the students actively opened the box, chose where to set it up, and established ways to manage sharing of this new resource. When the teacher announced that it was time to head to lunch, the students commented "It's time for lunch already?" (Pepe, 2015). The students' lunch time is 1:00 p.m. and their reply demonstrates a high level of engagement in their learning.

What has changed in the teaching and learning paradigm of this classroom? Learning has moved from teacher centered to student centered, beginning with flexibility. Pepe's role as a teacher has moved to one of a facilitator. She has found that she needs to be very flexible with what happens across the day, and planning has changed as well. With her team of teachers, the focus has moved to discussing the needs of students, how they can share ideas for target teaching, and how they can move students to other rooms to meet their needs. There is no need to create day-by-day plans for prescribed instruction and the covering of materials, plan the units or activities that end up with similar results, or have a homework plan for all students to complete the same homework. Digital tools, resources, and environments combine in Pepe's learning ecosystem to free teaching and learning from a set of standards in which all students perform the same task and move it to a more personalized constructive approach to learning.

In the School

Create the Raison D'être, or Reason for Being, for Your School

Take direction from Ray Trotter (2015):

> I also believe that it is essential that all schools have a clearly defined philosophical direction—a raison d'être—outlining significant aspects of their school's beliefs about teaching and learning, their organisational structures and learning environment, along with the school's approach to curriculum, leadership and

assessment. Without such a document it is extremely difficult for teachers to adopt a collective approach to teaching and learning across their school, or upgrade such practices as required. More importantly, unless a school knows where it wants to go, it doesn't matter which road it takes!

Make sure the map for your school includes enough flexibility in your organizational structure and learning environments to reach your teaching and learning goals. If they are misaligned, it will be difficult to reach established outcomes. Facilitate discussions and establish a plan on how to implement the use of flexible spaces, schedules, and roles to attain personalized learning opportunities for all students.

Educate and Involve the Parent Community

Duke School in North Carolina has a strong Parent Speaker Series, an educational forum that is organized by their Parent Service Organization. Their school and community are committed to the following vision:

> ... [P]reparing the next generation of problem solvers for our complex world. In doing so, we also acknowledge the challenges of today and the risk of unawareness. Renowned speakers, researchers, and educators inform, engage, and help families continue to raise responsible children and future leaders of America. (Duke School, 2015)

Don't risk "unawareness" with your parent community. Involve staff members in creating a plan to educate all stakeholders on new thinking in education and how it is playing out in your building. Host guest speakers and open up events to not only your community but also others. Designate a section of your website to capturing what is happening in your school with flexible spaces and schedules and how they impact learning. Include the voices of students and staff members, and support your updates with research. Hold symposiums at your school and showcase "flexible" examples in your building. Basically, promote how flexible spaces, schedules, and roles are transforming teaching and learning.

Create a Flexible Ecosystem Schoolwide

We cannot easily just get rid of classrooms, but we can redesign them to be used as learning studios and expand the learning into areas outside of the classroom walls. Making classroom spaces flexible within grade levels or across an entire building allows students to move through the total school environment to learn as needed. Involve staff members in creating a plan for your school that reflects a unified approach to a flexible learning ecosystem. Consider the following opportunities to be proactive in developing new areas and diverse forums for creative and entrepreneurial thinking:

- Can extracurricular activities be scheduled across the school day to drive interest in learning, instead of being available only before or after school?
- Have you turned your library into a learning commons, your computer labs into innovation labs, your outdoor spaces into learning or community gardens to grow business opportunities and increase engagement with experts, and so on?
- Does the school have flexible time and spaces, both virtual and physical, for collaboration and visible thinking?
- Is there ample space to build, experiment, and create?
- Is there common terminology for time to learn, such as WPPS's "learning agreement time"?
- Could you host Innovation Fairs, iLabs, Think Tanks, Do-It-Yourself events, Incubator Gatherings, or other types of activities?

In the School System

Offer Choice Within and Outside of District or System

Engage school leaders in discussions about the positive impact of flexible environments and roles leading to choice. Encourage schools to develop plans for their building as a school of choice and an option for utilizing flexibility in order to personalize learning opportunities. Choice is one of the four elements making up the Douglas County School District's Strategic Plan (2014):

> Matching children to the best learning environment: Choice creates the highest probability of success. In addition to school choices, we believe in choices within the classroom, choice pathways within a school, and even choices outside our own district if they are best for our students. According to Dr. William Glasser, all people have four basic needs—the need for love/belonging, power, freedom, and fun. Choice meets all four of these needs for our students and their families. In addition, choice and competition are important parts of continuous improvement. We learn from and are challenged by market forces associated with choice.

Choices within a district or system as well as outside are what will offer students the choice needed for personalized learning. School systems should create special academies to meet the needs of some students who have more unique needs that are not served in one place—science, technology, special education, and so forth. Students should also be given the opportunity to take courses offered through other schools or even establishments of higher education.

Rethink How Learning Is Scheduled and Offered

Learning is currently segmented based on the organization of an old system and typical requirements. Aligning how, when, and where learning takes place because of these old structures and assumptions will not get us to the level of autonomous learning that empowers students and offers the best influence to learners. Do all classes have to be 45 or 50 minutes long and span an academic term? Or, can learning take place for 5 minutes a day and last 4 weeks? Do all third-grade students need 6 weeks to learn multiplication facts? There is a current trend for "2-minute professional development," which exemplifies how we learn today as adults, and some of these same strategies could be applied for our students.

Create a Flexible and Personalized
Learning Ecosystem Systemwide

Systemwide change needs to foster personalized learning across all platforms for students and staff alike. Create flexibility and empowerment by implementing new policies and procedures that model the types of change desired. Professional development offered within or outside of the system should give credence to the use of flexible physical and virtual spaces and schedules, thus allowing teachers to negotiate their learning pathways.

Moving a district forward with unified platforms for digital technologies creates a fluid environment between what teachers do and how they can help students. For instance, offering Google Apps for Education on a districtwide basis ensures that teachers know how to use the tools they expect students to use.

REFLECTION

Our challenge as educators is to engage students in the learning that is relevant to them—to differentiate, to connect to their interests and passions, and to help them develop the skills they will need for their future career path. It is not easy to incorporate the time and freedom for this within the confines of our set schedules and designated places to learn. Discussions need to happen on many levels in order to change policies and procedures in an entire organization, and cost can be perceived as a deterring factor. Starting with small changes can have a huge impact, and it is possible to take on these challenges with minimal funding if teachers and schools concentrate on the most effective places. Redesigning classrooms as learning studios and repurposing and utilizing common areas allows for better teaching and learning. Expanding learning to outside areas whenever possible makes valuable connections to nature and fresh air. Empowerment can also be key—involving students in the process and giving them the freedom to take part in designing their learning spaces also inspires them to locate needed materials, furniture, and other resources.

Teaching is already a challenging and sometimes exhausting job, so it's understandable that teachers may also cringe at the thought of the time it takes and the management issues related to personalizing learning in a flexible environment. They can easily imagine the potential chaos of students being able to choose where and when they will create, collaborate, and learn. Within the framework of older paradigms in education, it is certainly difficult to imagine how to accomplish this task. However, with the benefit of new digital technologies, districts and organizations have made this more attainable. With increasing opportunities for online, blended, and adaptive learning, as well as the ease of access to information, students are able to take ownership for what and when they learn. Teachers utilizing current digital tools are empowered with multiple forums for increased communication, collaboration, and accountability. Shifting practice necessitates letting go of old paradigms, not just adding new ones on top of the old. Make sure to let go of the old in order to take advantage of innovative learning environments that are most conducive to relevant learning for today.

Activity #1: When, Where, and How Depends on What

Participants

Students, teachers, school administrative teams, or district-level educators

Objective

As we move to a naturally integrated approach to learning based on real-world projects and student passions, as opposed to subjects, it is important to gain an understanding of how optimal learning takes place. Depending on the specific outcome and the individual student, the *where*, *when*, and *how* of learning may vary. This activity will raise awareness as to the extent of flexibility needed to personalize learning that makes sense to the learner in a bigger, more relevant framework.

Materials

- Post-It notes in four colors

Process

Define the *what, when, where*, and *how*: Designate a different color post-it note for each of the following categories and have learners complete one or more for each. (15 minutes)

- On yellow . . . WHAT is a learning outcome you would like to pursue based on a personal interest or passion?
  - The outcome should have real-world applications.
  - The outcome could be a project or challenge.
  - The outcome could be a solution to a real-world need.
- On blue . . . WHEN would be the best time for you to pursue learning about this outcome?
  - Will you need to sequence various steps in the learning process?
  - Do you need to schedule time around a mentor or expert in the field?
  - Do you need to schedule interviews or meetings?
  - Are you scheduling with someone in another time zone?
  - Is the learning seasonal or dependent on a time of day?
  - Does the learning require repetition?

- On green ... WHERE would you need to be to best learn the outcome?
  - What are the places or digital spaces you will need to learn?
  - Do you need to travel to places or people?
  - Do you need to observe or collect data from a location(s)?
- On pink ... HOW would you learn?
  - Consider processes and tools.

Post and peruse: Post the completed notes by category in designated areas around the room (for example, yellow post-it notes on the front wall, blue post-it notes on the back wall, etc.). Have participants wander the room to view all of the responses. (20 minutes)

Analyze data: Divide the group into thirds and assign each group one of the following categories to discuss and analyze. (30 minutes)

- WHEN
- WHERE
- HOW

For each category, consider these questions:

- What do the data tell us about the need for flexibility in this category?
- What are some steps we can take to accommodate the various needs in a more flexible learning environment?
- How could you plan for these needs in a unit or term of study?
- How could some of the strategies suggested in this chapter be used to effectively manage the needs of the category?

Sum it up and share: Each group shares their findings and presents suggestions for planning and/or steps to take to accommodate this approach to personalizing a broad and flexible curriculum. (30 minutes)

ACTIVITY #2: ST-RE-T-CH IT OUT!

Participants

Teachers, school administrative teams, or district-level educators

Objective

Students have no problem working outside of the confines of a classroom, schedule, and dictated curriculum. It is teachers, schools, and the greater systems that have a harder time breaking out of these boundaries. In this activity, participants will analyze their current status and create a vision for stretching to a viable flexible educational environment leading to student autonomy.

Materials

- ST-RE-T-CH.pdf (a blank template for you to edit is available here: http://goo.gl/PjXH01)

Process

Individuals complete this process and then share with a partner. (60 Minutes)

Define and discuss: Provide copies or access to the ST-RE-T-CH pdf. (Participants may want to create a digital version of this on their own device.) As a group, define/discuss what each column designates and give examples of what that looks like for each row. (10–15 minutes)

Review, reflect, and rate as individuals: Pushing our practice towards student autonomy, our goal is to define what CHoice could look like in our learning environments. (20–30 minutes)

ST-RE-T-CH

Rate yourself on a flexible learning environment

	...STiff... Very structured routines Teacher/Systems Directed	...Redefining... Taking steps to make change Some student choice	...Testing... Implementing and reflecting Student/Teacher Co-create	...Choice... Options for learning abound Student Autonomy
Physical Space				
Virtual Space				
Schedules				
Teacher Role				

Follow these steps:

- Consider the examples given in this chapter and reflect on where they might fall on the chart.
- Complete the ST-RE-T-CH grid.
  - Place and describe your current status on the grid.
  - For each row, complete all sections to the right of your current status, listing descriptors of what this could look like in your educational environment or classroom. Think of this as a personalized rubric leading to choice for your specific situation.

Reflect

Discuss the following topics. (15–20 minutes)

- How will you achieve CHoice status?
- Was there something that surprised you?
- What challenges your thinking and/or your practice?
- In which area do you think it will be easiest to change?
- Will you sequence change in separate areas?
- Will changing one aspect dictate change in another . . . in all?

ACTIVITY #3: CREATE AN ECOSYSTEM FOR LEARNING

Participants

Students, teachers, school administrative teams, or district-level educators

Objective

A strategy that helps to better understand abstract concepts is the use of analogy. In this chapter, an analogy has been created between a biological ecosystem and a learning ecosystem. Participants will make comparisons and find similarities between these two dissimilar things in an attempt to better explain an effective learning ecosystem. They will then brainstorm ideas for an ecosystem that empowers student autonomy with flexible options for expanded learning applicable to their situation.

Materials

- Chart paper and markers
- Individual preference for note-taking and planning

Organization: Groups of four to six participants.

Process

Making connections: Complete the following steps. (30 minutes)

As a group, define *biological ecosystem*.

- What makes a healthy biological ecosystem?
- What contributes to an unhealthy biological ecosystem?
- Complete a chart with the following headings for a biological ecosystem:

Parts of a BIOLOGICAL Ecosystem	Healthy BIOLOGICAL Ecosystem	Unhealthy BIOLOGICAL Ecosystem

As a group, define *learning ecosystem* as explained in this chapter. Discuss how education is like a biological ecosystem.

- What makes a healthy learning ecosystem?
- What contributes to an unhealthy learning ecosystem?
- Complete a chart with the following headings for a learning ecosystem:

Parts of a LEARNING Ecosystem	Healthy LEARNING Ecosystem	Unhealthy LEARNING Ecosystem

Digging deeper: As individuals, think about your current learning ecosystem. Take time to reflect and brainstorm ideas to improve aspects of your individual learning ecosystem, moving it to a healthier environment that encourages a broad and flexible curriculum. (20 minutes)

Current Learning Ecosystem	Ideas to Make a Healthier Learning Environment

Sharing focus and forums: Discuss the following questions and complete the following activities. (20 minutes)

Our Focus

- How will you enhance or change your current learning environment?
- What are challenges in creating an effective learning ecosystem?
- What threatens the health of your learning environment?

Our Forums

- Physical dialogue: Reconnect as a group and share your thinking.
- Virtual dialogue: Share on a digital forum created for participants (Todaysmeet.com).

Future thoughts and follow-up: As a follow-up activity, participants could revisit the same Today's Meet, or a new one, and post the results of any changes they have made to their learning ecosystem.

REFERENCES

Douglas County Strategic Plan. (2014). Retrieved April 24, 2015, from https://www.dcsdk12.org/district/strategic-plan

Duke School. (2014). Parent Speaker Series. Retrieved April 24, 2015, from http://www.dukeschool.org/parentspeakerseries

Flick, L. (2014). Open Education Philadelphia—The Workshop School. Retrieved April 24, 2015, from https://vimeo.com/81754232

Hannon, V., & Patton, A., & Temperley, J. (2011, December). Developing an innovation ecosystem for learning. Retrieved from http://www.cisco.com/web/strategy/docs/education/ecosystem_for_edu.pdf

Nair, P. (2011, July 29). The classroom is obsolete: It's time for something new. *Education Week*. Retrieved from http://www.edweek .org/ew/articles/2011/07/29/37nair.h30.html

Pepe, A. (2015). Mrs. Pepe's class news. Retrieved April 24, 2015, from https://sites.google.com/a/dcsdk12.org/lte-grade-6/mrs-pepe-s-class/class-1-news

Perlman, B. (producer). (2012, April 27). Wooranna Park Primary School, tomorrow's school—short version. Retrieved April 24, 2015, from https://www.youtube.com/watch?v=uyeie_7EMp8

Thornburg, D. (2014). *From the campfire to the holodeck: Creating engaging and powerful 21st century learning environments*. San Franciso, CA: Jossey-Bass.

Thornburg, D. D. (2007, October). Campfires in cyberspace: Primordial metaphors for learning in the 21st century. Retrieved April 24, 2015, from http://tcpd.org/Thornburg/Handouts/Campfires.pdf

Trotter, R. (2015). What would a school built by Walt Disney look like? Retrieved April 24, 2015, from http://www.wooranna parkps.com.au/#!stimulating-learning-platforms/c1ifw

Tsai, C. (2013, February 13). If students designed their own schools . . . Retrieved April 24, 2015, from https://www.youtube.com/watch?v=RElUmGI5gLc

Wooranna Park Primary School. (2015). Personalising student learning videos. Retrieved April 24, 2015, from http://woorannaparkps .com.au/?page_id=33

Workshop School. (2015). Lighting 52nd Street. Retrieved September 6, 2015, from http://www.workshopschool.org/project/lighting-52nd-street/

Zhao, Y. (2012). *World class learners: Educating creative and entrepreneurial students*. Thousand Oaks, CA: Corwin.

7

Collaboration and Technology

Utilizing External Resources for Personalization

by Kay Tucker

Technology holds amazing potential to support the new paradigm of education in a number of ways. First, as a tool for creation, digital technology makes it much easier and less expensive to create media products and services. Second, as a tool of communication, technology enlarges the campus to make it possible for students to learn with experts and resources from outside the school. Third, as a platform for marketing, technology makes it possible for students to reach a global audience for their products. Finally, as a tool for collaboration, technology enables students to work with partners from around the world anytime from anywhere.

(Zhao, World Class Learners, *2012, p. 253)*

Featured School

Lone Tree Elementary, Lone Tree, Colorado

"For daily updates, follow us on Twitter and Instagram! @6PLTE." This invitation is centered on the classroom website of Alicia Pepe, a sixth-grade teacher at Lone Tree Elementary in Douglas County, Colorado. Alicia says that her personal approach to providing a world class education to her students "... combines several aspects including personalized, sustainable learning opportunities, technology integration, and restorative practices" (Pepe, unpublished work, 2015). In the following description of her approach, she illustrates a naturally integrated combination of technology with a personalized approach to learning:

> To approach mastery of Outcomes, students create personalized learning pathways for math and literacy to hone in on their strengths and passions, while mastering content. To create these pathways, they continuously analyze their data points from various assessments and create goals for themselves that are monitored and adjusted as needed. Doing so allows them to not only take a deep ownership in their learning, but also provides them the opportunity to pace themselves. Students pair with others that have chosen similar paths in order to collaborate and coach each other. This personalized learning has created more time in our schedule for students to receive targeted interventions to progress toward their goals. In addition, allowing students to choose how they would like to learn material, at what pace they would like to learn it, and in what format they will assess their understanding has created more sustainable learning. They also find the content more relevant and engaging and are able to demonstrate their learning more accurately than before.

> The use of technology has become second nature for us as we migrate to a paperless environment. Technology is not an optional tool in our room; it is required to provide our digital natives a World-Class Education. We are lucky to have several MacBooks, iPads, and Chromebooks for students to access

Google Apps, websites, and social media. Students utilize personal devices for research and creation of projects. Our class "pets" – robotic Spheros and Lego Robotics kits – are constantly in high demand as students play games or write code on iPads and computers to bring their creations to life. We create global connections with other classes and knowledgeable professionals using Skype or Google Chat. Students post on both Twitter (@6plte) and Instagram to capture what we are learning and their engagement in lessons. (Pepe, unpublished work, 2015)

Alicia Pepe had always effectively integrated technology into her classroom—"flipped" her class, connected to others via Skype, utilized technology for research and engagement, and allowed student choice in digital products. However, when she changed the focus in her classroom to a more student-driven approach to learning, she realized that it is not just technology integration that creates an innovative classroom.

This year, my greatest contribution and accomplishment has come from creating an empowering and flexible environment for my students that promotes student autonomy and personalized learning. In our classroom, instruction is personalized for the benefit of students; they are partners in creating their learning pathways as I have shifted my role from delivering content to facilitating quality learning experiences. (Pepe, unpublished work, 2015)

These quality learning experiences empower students to create and implement action plans for real-world projects. For instance, one group of students in Pepe's class is attempting to find a solution for the rising rental costs in Denver's housing market. In their learning experience, they have:

- Conducted research to study the effects of this problem and have chosen to help with the construction of a sustainable tiny house to provide a lower-income family the opportunity to live in an affordable home;
- Written several professional e-mails to adults outside the school asking for donations and information regarding their project;

(Continued)

(Continued)

- Contacted a building contractor who is familiar with the laws and techniques for building tiny houses and scheduled and conducted a face-to-face meeting with the contractor;
- Learned about sustainable energy options such as solar and wind power and the availability of such options in Denver; and
- Created blueprints for the construction of this home.

This one example shows how students script their learning pathways and networks as they use valuable skills and current digital technologies to solve real-world problems. The learning that happens along the way is relevant and meaningful to the students. As they master outcomes and content, the process is unique to them based on what they need to know, their level of understanding, and their personal goals. Making use of all possible digital technologies is necessary because it expands access to resources, increases the possibilities of collaborative efforts, and opens the door for students to connect and collaborate. The use of technology, as exemplified in this case, aligns to the thinking of Yong Zhao: If we use technology as a tool for creation, communication, and collaboration as well as a platform for marketing, it will lead to amazing results in the education of creative and entrepreneurial students.

PRINCIPLES BEHIND USING EXTERNAL RESOURCES TO PERSONALIZE LEARNING

The title of this chapter intentionally includes both terms *collaboration* and *technology*, because it is the combination of the two that brings about the possibility of using external resources to personalize learning experiences and, ultimately, lead to the reform that is envisioned in this book. Collaboration and technology combine to extend the limited exposure of a brick-and-mortar school to a world of learning outside of the classroom walls and outside of the realm of the teachers within a building. As teachers learn to facilitate this approach, student autonomy and personalized learning opportunities will come to life. The following are key actionable principles that are illustrated in this case:

- Commit to being connected and embrace new technologies.
- Co-create and contribute purposeful work to others globally.
- Create a framework of current digital tools mirroring real-world application.
- Empower students to drive how they use technology.
- Allow students to lead the way.

> The combination of the two—collaboration and technology—brings about the possibility of using external resources to personalize learning experiences and, ultimately, lead to the reform that is envisioned in this book.

Commit to Being Connected and Embrace New Technologies

(See Activity #1: #jointheconversation)

Teachers, classrooms, and students need to be connected to others globally—they need to use current communication tools in order to disseminate information, promote and receive ideas, engage in conversations, and gather feedback. What tools we use is not as important as the fact that we join the conversations about the things that we care about. Students need to be empowered at school with the tools they are already comfortable with (Instagram, Twitter, etc.), but they need to be taught how to use them intentionally as a vehicle for their learning. Students must also be taught to use these tools in a professional manner. If teachers model this approach in the classroom, it helps students gain an understanding of what it means to be a connected learner, as well as a connected citizen who participates ethically in global conversations and collaborative efforts.

Connecting as a teacher helps to understand the power of connecting our students. Teachers who have classroom Twitter and Instagram accounts linked to their websites immediately create transparent environments of the learning and sharing that goes on across the school day. They also create a bond with their students by communicating in a way that is natural and user-friendly to them. Alicia Pepe ties her sixth-grade Twitter and Instagram accounts together to function as one because this is a time-saving approach. How she uses these two forms of communication, with the same name of @6plte, accomplishes as much as, if not more than, a teacher posting pictures on a website or e-mailing families to showcase learning. The process of how Alicia Pepe broadcasts updates and news is completed quickly and easily without the need to be around a computer. Parents receive the visuals and information instantaneously, as they too are on the move and using mobile devices.

Creating a network of people—those you are "following" and those who are your "followers"—helps create a viable personal learning network. This is an informal learning network in which people connect with others with the specific intent that some type of learning will take place because of the connection. You may not know the people you are learning with and from, and chances are you may never meet them. Approaching a network as one from which you learn, as well as one to which you contribute, expands the network's effectiveness and the benefits, when considering learning opportunities, are greater. Think of the power of having students create networks based on their passions, strengths, and individual learning pathways. The potential for learning derives not only from learning from others as experts in an area but also from within the dialogue itself. The forming and sharing of opinions and fresh ideas will lead to the creativity and innovation that leads to entrepreneurial thinking—the thinking that will take them from consumers to producers.

Teachers are more apt to see the benefits of this kind of network for their students if they also participate in one. Recognizing the power of connecting helps teachers realize how important it is for each student to have his or her own personal learning network. At Lone Tree Elementary, both templates for the teacher digital portfolios and student digital portfolios include a page for a personal learning network (see the Resources for links to examples). The teachers' network is called a professional learning network (PLN), whereas the students' network is commonly called a student learning network (SLN). However, these terms all mean the same thing—having a network aligned with your learning objectives.

Alicia Pepe is comfortable with the use of current technology trends on a personal and professional level, and she documents her professional growth using a digital e-portfolio, participates in communities of practice on Google Hangouts, and follows hashtag (#) conversations on social media sites such as Twitter and Facebook. She has her own PLN, and continuous learning is possible via these social activities of peer-to-peer learning and online discussions using her mobile phone. The more comfortable teachers are in using apps and various software programs on a variety of digital devices, the more motivated they become to encourage students to do the same.

Co-create and Contribute Purposeful Work to Others Globally

(See Activity #3: Initiate a Global Project!)

> The more comfortable teachers are in using apps and various software programs on a variety of digital devices, the more motivated they become to encourage students to do the same.

[Introduction]

I was poking around on Twitter late one day,

When an idea popped in my head and made me say.

What would happen if we wrote a book?

One that would make the entire world take a look.

What if we had the world partake,

In a book project the world's kids would make?

So out of curiosity #TWIMA was formed,

A global project not like the norm.

SOURCE: Smith & McCool, *The World Is My Audience*, 2014. Reprinted with permission.

Co-creating, sharing, and learning from others around the world are activities in which we need to engage students. Just as important is the modeling of how to be the initiator of these global activities. Jon Smith, an educator in Canton, Ohio, initiated #TWIMA, which is an acronym for "the world is my audience." Based on the understanding that students produce better-quality work when they know someone other than their teacher will be viewing it, his main goal for publishing the global book *The World Is My Audience* was to broaden the scope of the audience for his students. In the description for the final product, Smith and McCool (2014) state that "In today's world with social media and global access to information, it only makes sense that children view the world as a place to share information and their work . . . I truly believe children will make and produce better writing when they can say, The World is My Audience."

Smith wanted to see how many classrooms he could get to work together on one project, so he began by "tweeting" out the idea and using a Google Form to gather interest responses. He received poems and artwork from 34 various places and is setting his sights on doing this again, with the goal of reaching even more global participants. Jon Smith sought out and found a group of teachers who collectively involved their students in an expressive project—definitely creative and collaborative—and one that served as a forum for diversity in thought and location. It connected students and the end result presented a global perspective.

Previously, teachers may have communicated with another classroom in which the teacher was an acquaintance, or a friend of a friend, or a family member. Classrooms may have communicated with another country if a parent had a connection in another part of the world. This was based on a very small network and limited ways of communicating. Teachers and students now have the possibility of online communities provided by third parties (e.g., iEARN, RandomKid, Flat Connections, etc.) to join in the efforts of projects created by others or to create their own projects. The exceptional thing available in our world today is the unlimited potential to reach out to an enormous amount of people with a simple tweet, Instagram photo, vine, YouTube video, and so forth. This alone allows for any one of us to spread our ideas, ask for involvement, or look for others as partners or customers.

The possibilities for connections and the ease of using new communication tools provide endless opportunities for collaboration and co-creation, and this is what needs to be part of every learning situation or classroom. Modeling how effective and easy it is to initiate a global conversation should be a process that all students, of any age, should understand. Imagine the excitement when a group of kindergartners see responses from around the world after they begin a hashtag (#) conversation about something they want to know more about. Once the group of students in Alicia Pepe's sixth-grade class complete their designs for a tiny house, imagine how easy it will be for them to begin the ripple effect of sharing their ideas, communicating needs, looking for partners requesting help, or gathering information. Once students are shown the power of this, they will only need to be given permission to connect with others—to find ways to bring people together from around the world to work collaboratively for the things they care about. We want our students to understand how to be the initiators, not necessarily the joiners, as they personally solve problems and take ownership for their learning and their actions.

Create a Framework of Current Digital Tools Mirroring Real-World Application

For quite a few years, the discussion has centered around 21st century tools, skills, and thinking. Considering the growth that has taken place since 2000 in the area of new technologies and the effects these technologies have had on changing how our world functions, one of the most obvious takeaways is that there will likely be many new technological options every day. What does this mean to an educator who is facilitating learning opportunities that are personalized and connected to real-world problems? It means that it is necessary to look beyond confining and/or typical educational software and platforms and look to real-world practices. What tools do entrepreneurs and corporations use? What tools help small businesses connect to a global audience? How do businesses grow their network and client base? How are data collected, managed, and used? How do people find work and understand needed job skills? How are innovative ideas being spread? How do partners and collaborators connect?

No matter what year it is, what month it is, or what day it is, the tools, skills, and strategies utilized for success in our rapidly changing world are also rapidly changing. The two go hand in hand. If we are to help students be successful, today as well as in the future, we need to open up possibilities for them that emulate a world that is rapidly evolving with innovation and change. This means we need to work in what might be called a time-sensitive mode and create an environment that does not use outdated material and old-fashioned strategies. Our classrooms and schools will go "stale" if we do not take proactive steps to stay abreast of current worldwide trends in technology and make connections to how these impact desired outcomes for our students. Knowing how to create and use networks, having the ability to perform tasks using multiple platforms, utilizing personal technology including mobile devices, creating multimedia, using social media to impact change, and utilizing the cloud for ease and security are all skills we want for our students.

One example of how Lone Tree Elementary is trying to emulate real-world technology and tools is by having all students create an online resume, similar to a LinkedIn profile but one that has been adapted for younger students. Students also establish a career pathway as early as first grade. Based on their interests and imaginations, the hope is students can envision themselves as being successful doing something they like, or they can design a job based on something they have created. By linking to online resources, fourth-grade students analyze both the businesses and entrepreneurs from the past that helped build Colorado. They have visited with local professionals and investigated current job opportunities (online) to help them look forward to and plan a pathway for their prospective career. The next step would be to use technology to connect to mentors and collaborators who have similar interests, or who could help them along the way in their quest for a future they are scripting.

Our world is driven by technology, and setting up a framework for success in this area means that educators should align "trending tools" with the desired skills and outcomes we want for our students. If the workforce is asking potential employees for a digital portfolio or a video resume, our students should know how to create these. Almost every business has a website, and our students should know how to build and script one. Because multimedia dominates our world with passionate and purposeful videos, our students should lead the way in making these. Online articles and blogs make thinking visible and draw attention to our new ideas and our causes. All students should have a visible presence and a strong digital footprint: Begin with student blogs. Conversations in our buildings and with our students should center on how technology is used in the adult world; how it enables creative thinking, communication, and collaboration; and how students can use, or create, the same or similar tools to create products or services and achieve their learning goals.

Empower Students to Drive How They Use Technology

Our students are ready and primed—they are not afraid to experiment with current technologies and they eagerly seek out new tools and experiences. This is what we want them to do, and our primary role in education should be to make sure they have what they need and want at their fingertips. It is no longer strategic for teachers to create confining lists of possible technology options, and it should never be said that choice equates to offering students different options as to the tool or program they use to show evidence of their learning. In a classroom where student autonomy is practiced in conjunction with real-world projects, the realm of technology will depend on the vision and outcomes as defined by the students. If students need a specific app downloaded on a school device or permission to download open-source software, they should be accommodated, as long as an adequate explanation is given as to how the new technology will align to meeting their goals.

Empower students to select and determine how they use technology in creating their learning pathway. Allow them to bring their own devices to school and use them. Many of Pepe's sixth-grade students have their own smartphones and they actively use them in purposeful ways across the school day. When the Lego robotics kit first arrived and students were excitedly constructing their first robot, several students grabbed their phones and immediately found and downloaded the necessary app enabling them to program and move the new creation from their individual phones. Another student in Pepe's class is planning to develop an app, and he has found several programs needed to write script. He didn't need to depend on his teacher to provide the right environment for his learning—he was simply given the permission to research, discover, and implement on his own using his own device or a school device. He was also given the name of a teacher in another building for the purpose of e-mailing her to coordinate a possible connection with her seventh- and eighth-grade students who participated in Verizon's Innovative App Challenge. Key here is that Pepe is not contacting the other teacher, and she is not the one researching what programs her student can use. The student himself is actively involved—both in using technology to connect to others as well as finding the appropriate digital tools in order to develop his ideas into a product.

Allow Students to Lead the Way

It is quickly becoming apparent in a paradigm in which teachers facilitate student learning that it is impossible to know everything our students ask of us. This is especially apparent in the field of technology. Coding, creating apps, robotics, writing script, and advanced ideas and questions aligned to a student's passions—these are all becoming frequent additions to student learning pathways. For these students, teachers' effectiveness will not be found in their ability to teach these concepts but it will be evident in their ability to:

- Connect their students to the appropriate resources for them to construct their own knowledge (mentors, You-Tube videos, apps, etc.),
- Allow them the freedom and time to pursue their quest for knowledge and to explore and apply their learning, and
- Create opportunities for students to teach each other on a global stage as well as in their own building.

When I was asked to provide examples to a group of teachers of how to bring robotics and coding alive in elementary classrooms, I answered that I would not be able to do this, but I had a group of students who could. In getting ready for the presentation, the students broke into several groups: one group who would showcase coding apps on iPads, another group who would demonstrate how to program the Lego Mindstorm robot, and a third group who could demonstrate how to program Spheros. These students then decided to create a website called Thrive Tech, which was to be used during the presentation but would continue on as a resource for "kids" and any interested teachers. Leading the way in this endeavor, this group of 12-year-old students embraced the idea that it was their charge to teach others the technology, not the charge of the teachers in the buildings across the district.

STRATEGIES FOR USING EXTERNAL RESOURCES TO PERSONALIZE LEARNING

In the Classroom

Create Classroom Social Media Accounts

(See Activity #1: #jointheconversation)

The favorite forums for social media are ever-changing, but the key is to pick the most current and most effective for your situation and for your audience. Think of how you personally like to receive information and you will quickly understand how your communities of students, parents, staff members, and/or peers want to receive information as well. Grab the attention of your stakeholders and your global audience by delivering short snippets of information with pictures and possible links to videos or longer articles. The audience with which we communicate is constantly on the move—they depend on their smartphones or mobile devices to keep up to date. They like to assimilate small engaging chunks of pointed information or media on a more frequent basis, as opposed to receiving lengthy e-mails or postings. This is what an Instagram or Twitter account will enable you to do.

Guarantee Student Access to Digital
Tools That Drive Personalized Learning

When the topic of conversation is about technology in schools, many scenarios arise. Our education environments may have the following:

- One-to-one computing
- Substantial amounts of technology, but home environments that do not have Internet access or devices
- Ample amounts of technology both at school and at home
- One iPad or one computer per classroom

Whatever the amount of technology, it should be used to support powerful new forms of learning—learning that can be personalized and adapted to students' goals, specifically, the individual goals of one student. Many times, technology and computer labs are used to accommodate all students doing the same thing at once—learning about or creating the same thing as a means of "teaching technology" or "teaching how to conduct a search." We do not want to use technology to teach in a one-size-fits-all approach; instead, we want to use it to open the doors for students to expand their unique passions and learning opportunities and to showcase what they create. Do we want all students following the same path of curated resources, or do want them to curate their own museum of resources based on what they are trying to achieve? Do we want all students to use the same software to create a final product that meets the requirements of a teacher-defined rubric, or do we want our students finding the tool of their choice that best allows them to create an innovative product or service? Whether students are using their own devices or you are sharing technology tools, try and figure out ways to focus on how these devices can drive a more personal approach to learning and an environment that supports student autonomy.

Create a Forum to Showcase Work Online

Expand the audience of your students. Similar to how Jon Smith wanted to create the idea for his students that the world is their audience, develop forums for your students to showcase what they are doing to a global community. Many forums exist, such as websites, Wikipedia sites, blogging sites for students (Edublogs or Kidblog), YouTube videos, and so forth. Choices abound—just make sure you pick one that will allow your students to have their voices heard and their creative ideas seen.

IN THE SCHOOL

Have All Teachers Create Professional Twitter Accounts

(See Activity #1: #jointheconversation)

Teachers should establish a professional Twitter account. This account should be separate from a personal or classroom Twitter account, because these accounts serve very different needs. A professional account enables educators to:

- Create a strong profile and establish a social media presence to connect and to showcase and get others excited about what they are doing;

- Personalize their professional development by purposefully following individuals or companies whose thinking aligns with theirs, which sparks an interest in learning more about a new topic of interest and pushes new ideas and current research; and
- Receive information that they want specifically pushed out to their staff by their own tweets or by the tweets of those mentoring staff members.

Implement Schoolwide Student Digital Portfolios

I created a possible template that is used by Lone Tree Elementary in all grade levels K–6. The template was created as a dynamic tool to drive personalized, product-oriented learning with areas for the following:

- Online resume: similar to a LinkedIn profile
- Career pathway: an area for students to share thoughts, show their links to their mentors, align their learning, reflect, and so forth
- Personalized learning plan: this section should be an ever-changing aspect of a student's learning with goals, action plans, links to resources, etc.
- Personal learning network: lists of who the student connects with to expand his or her learning aligned with the student's passions, strengths, and need to know

The portfolio is created in kindergarten and follows the student across all years at Lone Tree Elementary. The intent is not for the portfolio to be a dumping ground for completed work; rather, it serves as a tool for students and teachers to document goals and plans, passions and strengths, and links to possible connections and collaborations. The template should serve only to help guide teachers and students in the possibilities for a digital portfolio—it is not prescribed as something that should not be changed, and the portfolio is adapted to fit the needs of the individual student. Once it is downloaded, the student owns the portfolio and can revise it as needed to create a unique profile and tool.

Lead by Example With Connecting and Contributing

(See Activity #2: Connect and Contribute)

Connect With Others and Contribute Your Ideas!

Blog what you do best! Write articles for online publications. Contribute new ideas and spread your thoughts, gather feedback, reflect, and spread your thoughts again. This is a perfect cycle for innovation and design, and it is also a perfect cycle to expand thinking around the ideas and philosophies that promote schools of choice and drive commitment in our buildings. Discussion is so powerful, and it doesn't need to wait until newsletters, parent coffees, or professional development days. Break from the confines of your desk and spread the word about what is happening in your building. There is something powerful that happens with the process of visible, passionate, and purposeful communication. Expressing ourselves to an expanded audience as educators is as impactful as expanding the audience for our students. Everyone brings their best game when they have more followers or the gallery is greater.

Contribute Resources to Enable Others to Connect!

As a school, model how to connect and use new technologies to impact positive change in developing countries. No matter how restricted we feel with our resources, there are others who have less. There are many opportunities for schools to connect with other schools and at the same time expand the learning opportunities for their own students. The following are two possible examples:

- TEDx in a Box: This resource is "[d]esigned by consultants at IDEO . . . [and] contains everything needed to host a TEDx event: a projector, subtitled TED talks, a sound system, microphones and a how-to guide."
- LumenEd: LumenEd connects students in classrooms around the world in a video pen pal program. The LumenEd Bright Orange Box projector " . . . allows teachers to teach, and students to learn, without worrying about Internet access, electricity, or anything else."

In the School System

Accelerate Personalized Learning With
Systems in Place for BYOD Programs

Creating procedures and initiatives for Personally Owned Devices (PODs) or Bring Your Own Device (BYOD) programs could have the single biggest impact on personalizing learning, and one of the largest current trends in growing technologies is in the area of mobile computing devices. Take advantage of both of these and put systems in place that empower students to bring their own digital devices to school. Personalized learning may be facilitated in many ways, but the possibilities for successful impact are accelerated when students are able to use their own digital devices. Similar to how adults personalize smartphones or personal computers to help pursue their passions, accommodate for organizational needs, or meet the needs of their professional challenges, students benefit from the same approach. The advantage to schools is twofold—it transfers the responsibility for maintenance of the device to the owner and offers more flexibility in accessing differentiated global resources and tools for the student. Lone Tree Elementary initiated a POD program in 2011 after it was defined and supported on the district level. The Douglas County School District established the expectations and their IT department established minimum system requirements, making it easy for schools to implement it when they were ready.

Provide Consistent Systemwide
Digital Tools, Access, and Procedures

Gone are the days where teachers and students save their work on a specific machine or have to be on campus to access a server—now we have the cloud. Google Apps for Education is one example of a universal tool that allows organizations to expand their boundaries so that all users are not limited in their ability to complete their work. They can collaborate in real time with their peers or with others from around the world. Whether you provide Google Apps for Education or another form of accessible cloud-based applications, these tools should:

- Enable both teachers and students to create sustainable learning experiences that access a global platform of information and participants,
- Provide communication and collaborative tools that are used on a global basis, and
- Emulate tools that are used in the workforce.

Another challenge for districts or large educational systems is to provide Internet access that is universal so that running all of these devices and programs will not falter. Funding and establishing this should be at the forefront when prioritizing expenditures.

Replace Professional Development Courses With
Continuous Learning Opportunities and Performance Support

A trend to be considered is to change how we conduct professional development in our organizations. Learning at a moment of need is crucial for teachers, and it is possible in our connected world. Consider the value of a learning environment that is both personalized and continuous for teachers—taking place over the course of a semester, year, whatever it takes. The dialogue and ongoing learning is supported by a facilitator, mentor, or coach who offers active performance support. Performance support means that the teachers are assisted as they implement change or new ideas in their learning environments—they are not sent out the door after a 15-hour course with the hopes that they will shift their practice based on a one-time professional development course.

This approach has been effective at Lone Tree Elementary. In previous years, teachers have taken courses aligned to the district's vision and/or interests of the individual teachers. The courses were viable and connected to shifting practice to new paradigms in education; however, the impact of these courses was not as noticeably evident as when the school took a personalized approach to professional development. Now teachers interact continuously via Google Apps or by social media and pertinent articles and ideas are shared with specific teachers or teams ready to move in new directions. The leadership team is constantly on the move, giving performance support as needed when new ideas are implemented. Change spread rapidly based on this personalized approach and was much more significant than any change created by teachers attending a one-time course.

REFLECTION

Educational technology has been disrupting educators, policy makers, parents, and students for at least the past 20 years and the scale of change it has brought about is enormous. Basically, technology has revolutionized the learning process. However, it has prompted many controversial conversations and questions:

- Is informal learning as valuable as formal learning?
- Where should learning take place?
- If we can "Google it," should we teach it?
- Should students use their mobile devices in class?
- How do we support new technologies both financially and with training in schools?

Even though quality learning experiences are greatly enhanced and accommodated by the use of technology, these discussions continue. If we step away from a fear of change and move forward with the concept of student autonomy and personalized learning pathways with teachers as facilitators, we find ourselves acknowledging that technology needs to be ubiquitous and that it is the key to empowering our students. In describing her students, Alicia Pepe said: "They are partners in creating their learning pathways as I have shifted my role from delivering content to facilitating quality learning experiences" (Pepe, personal communication, 2015). Without technology, this approach of student-driven learning and collaborative efforts would not be possible.

Activity #1: #jointheconversation

Participants

Teachers, students, school administrative teams, or district-level educators

Objective

Teachers and classrooms need to be connected and use current communication tools in order to disseminate information, promote and receive ideas, engage in conversations, and gather feedback. Not only does this help to gain an understanding of the process, but it also models for educators and students how to use these tools in a purposeful and professional manner. In this activity, participants will accomplish the following:

- Create a classroom/school/administrative Twitter profile if applicable
- Create a professional Twitter profile
- Add apps to mobile devices as needed
- Follow pertinent people to personalize the experience
- Join or start a conversation

Materials

- Digital devices with Internet access and mobile devices (phones, iPads)
- Paper to list/brainstorm who to follow

Process

Organization: Individual activity with group discussion and peer mentors to help set up accounts and tweet.

Overview of how Twitter is a tool to personalize learning: Follow a professional Twitter account (@Edutopia, @Mind ShiftKQED, etc.). Follow an educator's Twitter account. For example, our authors' accounts are: @etiltucker, @grs haid, @emilymccarren, and @growingupglobal. Check out the profile. Who is this person/organization following? (10 minutes)

Who would you follow? Discuss and share at your table examples of organizations or professionals that you would like to follow in order to be informed of their ideas or conversations. For example: @YongZhaoUO. (10 minutes)

Create and follow: Sign up and create a profile for your account. Begin entering people you would like to follow. (20 minutes)

What's trending? Check out current conversations: #yongzhao. (10 minutes)

Have a real conversation! (10 minutes)

- How can a Twitter account be used for personalized professional development or student learning?
- How could your students, class, staff, or system begin a conversation that would be beneficial to them?

Reflection

Now that you are using Twitter in your classroom or for professional development, answer the following:

- Does this tool serve a viable purpose for you and/or your stakeholders?
- Could you expand how you use this tool?
- How many people are following you and how many people are you following?
- Is your profile still accurate?

ACTIVITY #2: CONNECT AND CONTRIBUTE!

Participants

Teachers, school administrative teams, or district-level educators

Objective

Expressing ourselves to an expanded audience as educators is as impactful as expanding the audience for our students. By doing ourselves what we know is best for our students, we cement our understanding in what it means to communicate on a global stage—what it means to contribute our ideas to others. Participants will brainstorm ideas on how to lead by example as they connect with others and contribute their ideas.

Materials

- Digital devices with Internet access
- Paper to list/brainstorm who to follow

Organization: Individual activity with group discussion.

Process

What could I contribute? Individually, brainstorm a list of things that could inspire you to connect and contribute on a global stage. (10 minutes)

- I would like to spark change by . . .
- I would like to gather more information from others about . . .
- I feel confident in sharing my strengths in . . .
- I am passionate about . . .

Share: All participants in the group/at the table share one thing on their list that they could contribute to and benefit from by joining an expanded conversation. (10 minutes)

How can I connect and contribute? As a group, discuss all of the possibilities for contributing to global conversations. (10 minutes)

- Do different topics benefit from specific forums?
- Does participating across multiple forums benefit you as the contributor?

Reflection

After you have connected and contributed on a global stage, reflect on how this has impacted you as an educator.

- Did the process solidify your thinking or expand your thinking?
- What have you learned about yourself?
- What have you learned about this process and how it could benefit your staff or your students?

ACTIVITY #3: INITIATE A GLOBAL PROJECT!

Participants

Teachers, students, school administrative teams, or district-level educators

Objective

Co-creating, sharing, and learning from others around the world are activities in which we need to engage students. Just as important is the modeling of how to be the initiator of these global activities. Technology opens up endless possibilities to collaborate on projects and co-create products or services. This activity helps participants define possible projects to initiate based on the desired outcomes for their students and possible strategies for implementation.

Materials

- Chart paper and markers

Organization: Groups of three to four participants, based on job assignments.

Process

Reread: Refer to the section starting on page 161 on how to co-create and contribute purposeful work to others globally. As a group, discuss the following topics. (10 minutes)

- Why was #TWIMA created as a global project?
- What did it accomplish?
- How were students impacted by this project?

Brainstorm ideas of possible global projects: Using the chart paper and markers, list ideas for global projects that would work in your learning situation. Consider a broad integrated context for learning and exposure to a diverse mix of ideas and/or cultural elements. (20 minutes)

Choose one to implement and create a plan to initiate: Select from the following. (20 minutes)

- Make a group decision as to which one to implement.
- Create a plan to initiate.
  - What is the final project?
  - How will you connect to collaborators?
  - What tool will be used to create the projects?
  - How could students/staff be involved?
  - How will the final project be shared?

Share: Share your plan with the larger group. (10 minutes)

Reflection

After initiating a global project, reflect on the following:

* What impact did the project have on your students/ staff?
* What feedback have you received about the final product?
* What would you do differently if you initiated another project?

REFERENCES

Pepe, A. (2015, January 7). Grant application for Apple awards (unpublished)

Smith, J., & McCool, E. (2014, December 1). *The world is my audience.* iTunes description. Retrieved April 27, 2015, from https:// itunes.apple.com/us/book/the-world-is-my-audience/ id947404869?mt=11

Zhao, Y. (2012). *World class learners: Educating creative and entrepreneurial students.* Thousand Oaks, CA: Corwin.

RESOURCES

Lone Tree Elementary. Student digital portfolio template. Retrieved from https://sites.google.com/a/dcsdk12.org/lte-portfolio/

Lone Tree Elementary. Teacher digital portfolio template. Retrieved from https://sites.google.com/a/dcsdk12.org/lte-professional-eportfolio/

LumenEd. Retrieved from http://LumenEd.org

Project #TWIMA. Retrieved from http://mrsmithtrt.weebly.com/ project-twima

TED. TEDx in a Box. Retrieved from https://www.ted.com/about/ programs-initiatives/tedx-program/tedx-in-the-developing-world/tedx-in-a-box

Tucker, K. Lone Tree Elementary student digital portfolios. Retrieved from: https://sites.google.com/a/dcsdk12.org/lte-portfolio/ home

8

Autonomy With Responsibility

Preparing Ethical Entrepreneurs

by Emily McCarren

In a world where human interests, backgrounds, living conditions, and abilities are diverse, it is ethically wrong and economically disastrous to reduce all the diversity into a few skills. Granting and supporting individual students' pursuit of learning enables the development of unique and diverse talents.

(Zhao, World Class Learners, *2012, p. 238)*

Financial profit does not have to be the sole pursuit of an entrepreneur. Social entrepreneurship, for example, aims to create social values, benefits to society, rather than financial values.

(Zhao, World Class Learners, *2012, p. 77)*

Preparing students with the skills and the ethical dispositions to invent a future that enhances human well-being in this space of possibility is the most critical challenge for schools in our time.

Fernando Reimers

Featured School

Entreamigos, San Pancho, Mexico

The Entreamigos community center is housed in a repurposed milk processing plant in San Pancho, Mexico. Today the space teems with life and energy as community members of all ages come to use the library, computer lab, art studios, classrooms, exercise spaces, and recycling center. In 2006, the center's founder, Nicole Swedlow, rented a small storefront in her adopted hometown of San Pancho, Mexico. With a background in arts education and a hankering for social change, she envisioned a space in which local community members could exchange knowledge: She could teach arts and crafts, and others could share their strengths and gifts—cooking, other practical skills, language lessons, and so forth. In Spanish, "entre amigos" means "between friends."

As community members began to frequent her storefront, Nicole heard more and more of their stories: of the local schools that suffered from high teacher turnover and low retention, and of young adults with remarkable local knowledge who were unemployable in the new tourism economy because they spoke only Spanish. She also began to see the clear divisions between the expats who had come to San Pancho for the relaxed way of life it provided and the local people who created and established that way of life. The vision for Entreamigos was born—a place where the knowledge of the community and the worth and dignity of each individual was to be celebrated and shared, on equal footing. It didn't matter if you lived in a beachfront home or in a humble shed on the street behind the building itself—everyone had something to teach and learn.

Indira, an art educator with a particular passion for recycling, was one of the first employees that Nicole had in the community center. Nicole and Indira began brainstorming ways to improve their beloved community together. A townwide recycling program is one of several impactful things that grew out of their work. Through Indira's passion and Nicole's support, residents of San Pancho can now recycle most of their household waste that previously would lie in their yards until a good rain would wash it out to sea. In her art classes with local children, Indira began to explore the idea of reusing some of the waste prior to recycling it. Adults began creating beautiful toys for the younger children in their families out of used detergent bottles and other recyclable plastic. Waste was transformed into wonder and the children began to become the agents of change in their community by cleaning out their yards to bring more supplies to the community center, from which to make art. When Nicole tells this story, she is quick to say that this passion was Indira's, not hers, but because she nurtured it and created space for Indira's passion to flourish, the seed of an idea grew into something meaningful. The ethical norms of Entreamigos are clear: They believe in caring for the shared earth and the children in the community and they believe that every member of the community has something to share—every action is based on this ethical foundation.

Entreamigos was born out of the entrepreneurial spirit of an individual, and it has been an amazing success in that it has created a space in which learners of all ages can explore their own passions and thrive. The purpose of this chapter is to help readers consider ethics as they relate to highly personalized learning environments. First, we explore what ethics means in this realm—that "personalization" does not mean solely for personal benefit. Students must build on and nourish their strengths for the good of others. In doing so, their learning will be well served. We also discuss the ways in which the tenets of entrepreneurship can be reclaimed from the business world, which can tend to have negative connotations, particularly for educators.

Entreamigos is not a school in the traditional sense, and it is therefore liberated from some of the constraints that schools can experience. They have no mandated curriculum, no predetermined standards or outcomes. But Entreamigos is doing many of the things that schools need to do: It is examining the needs of the community and responding with creative and entrepreneurial solutions that leverage the strengths, passions, and talents of individuals, creating room for all community members to grow and thrive. All of the educational and pedagogical shifts discussed

(Continued)

(Continued)

in this book (and any educational reform or change efforts) mean nothing if they are not rooted in a strong ethical foundation. To understand what this means, we can consider the following questions:

- How do our students make decisions about what is right and what is wrong?
- How do our students define ethical behavior and action?
- What is the role of each class or teacher in developing these skills?
- What kind of people do we want our students to be?

In a school focused on personalization, questions like these can become the throughline of a student's experience. Students creating social good becomes a desired outcome of schooling.

PRINCIPLES FOR ETHICS IN PERSONALIZED LEARNING

One of the greatest challenges in personalized learning is the misunderstanding that personalization is all about the individual's self-interest without considering the needs of others or the broader good of the community and environment. The truth is that personalization necessitates collaboration, and sustainable entrepreneurial activities require caring about others (and their environment) and seeking to serve their needs. Personalized learning is not isolated learning. Personalized learning should not be a lonely endeavor. On the contrary, in a thriving personalized learning environment, the learners are in constant connection with other learners, exploring and seeing the many ways that a community with diverse talents, strengths, and passions can go about making the world a better and more interesting place.

Aristotelian ethics taught that self-knowledge is the foundation of a meaningful life, a life that will effectively serve others. By creating opportunities for students to discover and nurture their own strengths and interests, we are developing students with strong self-knowledge. Once that foundation is built (and continues to be rebuilt over the course of a life), students must have the opportunity to explore ways in which their gifts will serve the needs of others.

Ethics are in fact the boundaries in personalized learning environments, and ethical behavior and action are the limits for highly personalized learning. A student asks, "What should I do, teacher?" And a teacher responds, "You should do what you care deeply about and seek to make positive change in that realm." One of teachers' common criticisms of highly personalized learning, as it relates to students, is that "They can do anything! There are no limits, no boundaries." This is not true. This notion of service to others helps to create a structure: Students can do anything—that will be in service to others for greater social good.

Teachers and instructional leaders must create opportunities for students to learn that serving others is the purpose of all good work and collaboration is mutually beneficial. This begins with empathy, an essential skill in any century (although it has been heralded as an especially essential skill in this one). Empathizing with the needs of others, and finding ways that your skills, talents, and interests can meet the needs of others is what school should be about. As educators, our job is to find ways to engage authentic audiences with our students in ways that serve our students' learning as well as the audience.

GREEN INVENTIONS AND SUSTAINABLE ENTREPRENEURSHIP

At the core of entrepreneurship are the wants and needs of people. In order to create anything that people will purchase, use, subscribe to, or believe in, entrepreneurs need to understand the needs and wants of their target market, audience, or users.

The relationship between sustainability and entrepreneurship has not always been clear. Sustainability has come to connote environmental preservation and restoration—with the idea that this is an essential effort with which all people on this planet should be engaged. Students and teachers need to understand this important connection between entrepreneurship and sustainability as they create and engage in learning opportunities. For enterprises—even business enterprises—to succeed in the long run, they must care about others and the environment.

Social Entrepreneurship

Social entrepreneurship, an endeavor that seeks innovative solutions to social problems, is a concept that has been gaining traction in popular and academic discourse. It is also a movement with great traction among young people, in part due to underemployment of many millennials. Because many students are leaving school and are not able to find the traditional jobs that school has prepared them for, the most motivated young people are creating their own new jobs. And this is not just a concept for nonprofits and students. In the *Journal of Business Ethics*, Felipe Santos asserts that social entrepreneurship has become "an important economic phenomenon at a global scale" (2012, p. 335). Schools need to shift to prepare students to develop their capacities to be meaningful social entrepreneurs. Although not all student work can be labeled as social entrepreneurship, it should always be used as a goal that we are working toward.

The relationship between entrepreneurship and ethics is not always obvious; the link between the two is essential to understanding the role of educators in this paradigm of education. An opinion piece by David L. Kirp (2014) in the *New York Times*, titled "Teaching Is Not a Business," was widely circulated by educators and noneducators alike. The article describes the distance between the cold, faceless tactics and practices of business and the highly personal and relational work of teaching and learning. Historically, entrepreneurship has been associated with business in which success is measured by profit margins. However, entrepreneurship is a concept that is highly personal and relational—it is about identifying people's needs. Education in general and educators in particular tend to recoil from any suggestion that links their field to business terminology or strategies. A social entrepreneur, however, is an individual who uses the same entrepreneurial mindset that makes businesses succeed (seeing opportunity in challenges, thinking creatively and divergently, and seeing new possibility in the common) to affect positive and meaningful social change. Success is measured by value added to a community, and not exclusively by profit margins. In many ways, the concept of entrepreneurism needs to be reclaimed—taken back from the grasps of profit-driven, loosely ethical endeavors. This is not to say that social entrepreneurship does not result in profits—it absolutely can and does. Although media reports tend to highlight the exceptions, most businesses operate from a strong ethical foundation. Our work in schools is to inculcate that and make sure that students know it is important.

As personalization becomes the default in your class and school, it creates a remarkable space to engage students more deeply in the work of becoming a social entrepreneur. As entrepreneurial educators, we have the opportunity to inculcate the sense that serving the needs of others is not something that we do just to serve; rather, understanding the needs of others—empathy—is central to success in any field, from health care and law to science, marketing, or education. Any career imaginable (and even those yet unimagined) will be well served by an individual who is able to identify a need and design a solution for that need. However, our schools generally do not yet seem to help our children develop such skills and values.

Grades Versus Humanity

Research suggests that students in the United States care more about achievement in school than caring for others, and that they believe that their teachers and parents also value achievement over being good people (Weissbourd et al., 2014). According to the study, students believe that it is more important to their teachers and parents that they get good grades than act as good people. Of course, teachers and parents don't feel that way—according to their data, both parents and teachers believe that the most important thing is nurturing students to become happy and caring adults. The troubling reality is that students perceive that teachers and parents value achievement above caring. This is a devastating disconnect in our schools.

Although educators may feel that we let students know what we value and we help them develop a strong sense of ethics (and some of us might be successful at this), the research suggests that overall in the United States, educators (and parents) are not effectively communicating our beliefs and values to our students. We may be saying that ethical behavior and caring for others is important and we may have rules to enforce associated norms, but there is a disconnect between what we say and believe and students' perception about what is important to us. School cultures tend to prize achievement above all else. We do not often enough engage our children in activities that enable them to learn about others, enjoy helping others, and understand human interdependence. The Harvard Graduate School of Education's Making Caring Common Project seeks to help schools by sharing strategies for emphasizing the values that mean the most to us in schools, so that kids can learn from what we believe and our actions as school leaders and educators can demonstrate and align more closely with our values.

Nicole identified a need in San Pancho. Now, children in her community are challenged to ask the same questions: Why do I matter? How can I be of value to others? What are my passions and how can they serve my community? People want to be useful to others. Entreamigos functions like a school. Nicole has set the ethical constraints of the projects in which her learners can engage, such as building toys for local children from recycled materials, supporting robust after-school programs, or creating a community recycling program. Nicole created the space in which these activities could happen.

She did not tell the people who came to the community center what to do; rather, she expressed that the mission and vision of the center was to serve all of the members of the community, and then the members of the community engaged in highly personalized paths of filling that need in diverse and exciting ways. In a more traditional classroom setting or school, these same ideas can apply. Again, not all work in schools should lead to social action, but more of it would be a great service to our students and the world they will inherit.

Community Service and Engagement

Education in general, and civics classes and community or service learning programs in particular, has long challenged students to be engaged and informed participants in their society. Looking at this form of engaged participation through the lens of social entrepreneurship gives new life to this concept. When our schools give significantly more time and space to personalization (the opportunity for our students to identify, find, and explore their passions), the outcomes of schooling will more closely match our lofty ambitions. In most schools, the notion of community service lies on the margins of the curriculum. Some schools require a certain number of hours, whereas others weave work in the community into course requirements. However, few schools articulate that the purpose of this work is to add value to the community: not just to spend hours, but to effect change.

Our education systems (schools, community centers, and homes) have the potential to produce young adults who all feel not only empowered but also obligated to make changes for the social good in their communities. Their work in their elementary, middle, and high school experience must give them opportunities to act on things that they care about and to effect social change. In our classrooms and schools, the process of ethical entrepreneurship begins with empathy: the ability to understand and share the feelings of another. If our students develop and practice the skill of empathy and we use that as a point of departure in their learning, the possibilities are endless. Schools have long understood the value of empathy and community connection. Service learning is an effort to acknowledge the bidirectionality of this type of learning. With community service, the assumption is that the receptors of the service are benefiting from the benevolent servers. A shift toward the notion of service learning begins to acknowledge that it is through service—and that deep engaged empathy that accompanies well-crafted service learning opportunities—that students learn best. With any term applied to this practice, there is an assumption that the action will benefit both the server and the served.

By bringing service learning and community service to the core of what we do in schools, we can increase opportunities for our students to understand the fundamental notion of the worth and dignity of each individual in our community. Similarly, we honor the worth and dignity of each of our students by giving them the opportunity to serve others with their gifts, interests, and strengths.

Hazards of Thoughtless Community Involvement

It is not enough to say that our students should have an impact on the community and let them loose. Although there is little doubt that this will increase engagement and learning for the students, educators have an obligation to do everything they can to ensure that there is no harm done to the community in the course of their students' work. Satirical expressions such as "voluntourism" and the overtly negative "poverty safari" describe the unproductive and often damaging end of the spectrum of service learning. These terms satirize the danger in overemphasizing the benefit of service for the volunteer while minimizing (or worse, ignoring) the potentially negative impact that it can have in a community.

One example is the story of a well-meaning group of students and educators from an independent school that traveled to India and built a home in a small village. Shortly after they took their pictures with village children, updated their Facebook profiles, and boarded the plane home, a corrupt government official took over the house from the family the students thought they were building it for, locked it up, and tried to sell it for a profit. For students to engage meaningfully in a community (whether in their backyard or on the other side of an ocean), they (and their teachers) must be well prepared to really understand what their presence will mean in the community in which they are working.

Cultural Contexts in Communities

As our students venture into the space of working toward change in their communities, they will begin to challenge all sorts of community and cultural norms. Challenging norms is not always simple, or even positive—particularly when looked at in a historical, social, or political context. For example, at an international school in Korea, a group of students organized a campaign based on their beliefs and passions. The topic of interest to them was the practice of eating dog meat. They sought to convince community members that this practice was repulsive and encourage (and shame) them to choose a different protein source. By many of the concepts outlined thus far in this book, this was a great project. Individual students found a topic that they were passionate about and wanted to change, they were researching and planning how to do it, and they were supported in this process by teachers who had created a sense of responsibility for positive social change. But was this project ethical or rooted in empathy? Had the students considered the long history of dog consumption in Korea? Had they explored the fact that there is a distinction between dogs raised for meat and dogs raised as pets? Had the students gone out into the community to understand the extent to which this work was needed?

Regardless of your opinion of the practice of consuming dog meat, the example brings up compelling questions about how we define ethical entrepreneurship. Do our students design projects and inquiries that benefit people? Do they carefully and deeply consider the cultural, social, political, and linguistic realities of the people that they are working with? This is hard work! In this type of a learning environment, the role of teacher (as described in previous chapters) will feel more like counselor, consultant, and advisor than what we may have experienced in student-teacher relationships in our own schooling or in our career as educators up to this point. For many educators, the role of fostering ethical entrepreneurs in our classrooms and schools is uncharted territory.

Autonomy, Responsibility, and Right

In the Hawaiian language, the word for responsibility is *kuleana*. It has a deeper meaning than its English counterpart because in addition to responsibility, kuleana also means "right," as in something that you deserve to be able to do. There is a great deal of power in this word in Hawaiian communities because it seems to be connected to something from long ago but is quite forward looking at the same time. At this moment in time, both educators and students globally have a significant kuleana. Teachers are working in a time that allows them to connect their students' passions, strengths, and interests to their learning in ways that have never before been possible. Through technology, we can connect our students to the world and give our students the opportunity to collaborate, make meaning, and share their powerful voices with global audiences. It is our kuleana, our right and our responsibility, to provide this for our students.

STRATEGIES FOR PREPARING
ETHICAL ENTREPRENEURS

In the Classroom

Co-Create Shared Norms (Thinking: Beginning)

What does it look like to establish a culture of social entrepreneurship in our classrooms? Some of the teachers who are best at this can be found in early elementary school classrooms, where there is often a culture of crafting classroom "rules" together. The earlier students engage (and have agency) in questions surrounding what type of community we want to have, the better. This same process throughout the middle and high school years is equally valuable, yet it is practiced much less often. Teachers should nudge students to come to increasingly sophisticated understandings of what it means to behave and work ethically in a particular classroom or school. This will then inform the way students behave and how they choose to impact the broader community. At Aspirations Academies in the United Kingdom, students are considered genuine partners in the governance of the school, and of course the classrooms. Within classes, individual students can apply for the position of subject partners. In a high school class, a history teacher's subject partner sits with the teacher during lesson planning and assessment and gives feedback— not on the content, but on the ways that the students are being taught and engaging in the community. This is the organization's way of ensuring student voice in the classroom.

Leverage Case Studies (Thinking: Beginning)

Learning through case studies is a method that is employed in many professional fields (e.g., law, medicine, and educational leadership), and this can be a wonderful tool in classrooms as well. Have students create stories of unethical behavior that they notice in their school or community, and then invite them to present and debate the cases in class. They could do this with writing, role playing, or video projects.

Create Change Agent Projects (Implementing: Intermediate)

In your class, think about how you can make space for students to have meaningful and positive impacts in their local, national, or global community. Don't fall into the trap of assigning students a project and then determining the outcome— make sure the product and the audience is authentically theirs. Even if you have learning outcomes such as a particular math or scientific concept, challenge your students to figure out a way to have an impact with this knowledge. Maybe they can tutor students at your school or local schools. Maybe they can then make a play or write a children's book about the concept and present it to a retirement community or a preschool. Maybe they can then take on some more research and spend time in a lab in the community volunteering their time to advances in a related field that is of interest to them.

In addition, the skills that your students are learning may be of interest to schools in other parts of your local community or perhaps in other parts of the world. For example, if you are a world language teacher and teach Mandarin Chinese, perhaps your students could expand their own self-knowledge by making videos designed for Chinese tourists to showcase things the students are passionate about in your community. In this case, students are charged with creating a product for an audience that might not otherwise be served, heard, or supported. These are the constant questions that ramble in the minds of world class educators: What are the opportunities for my students learning to serve, and be served by the needs of others? Can their work improve the world?

Reimagine the Expectations (Expanding: Advanced)

In a middle or secondary school, collaborate with other teachers and relieve students of other requirements in your classes if they are working on a social entrepreneurship project. Be creative and flexible about requirements in your class. If you are an English teacher, accept reflections about their work or press releases that they write about their services or products that they are developing in lieu of term papers or in class exams.

Give Students Voice (Expanding: Advanced)

After thoughtful discussions about the worth and dignity of each individual, let your students know that they will be determining their own grade in your course. Work with them to develop a shared understanding of your co-created expectations and then let them be reflective of their own work. This can be a complex thing, particularly in a school where grades are highly valued. However, in the experience of Paula Hodges, the assistant principal and science teacher at Punahou School, when teachers use this method, students tend to value the opportunity and are often more reflective and self-critical than if they were simply the recipients of grades from the teachers.

In the School

Let Students Lead (Implementing: Intermediate)

Building on norms about interpersonal behavior is a great place to start. For example, we hope that our work will not profit at the expense of others, that we will care for those in need of our care, and that we will treat others as we would want to be treated. Many schools attend to this on a school-wide basis through honor codes, character education programs, or peer-counseling training programs.

With a schoolwide honor code, or council, students can become engaged in defining and establishing the ethical norms of the community—this could be through a special group, or we could give the traditional student government more of an authentic role in this work than most have. Like many other boarding schools, the Thacher School in Ojai, California, has a committee of students and faculty members that hears student discipline cases. The committee's role is to make a recommendation about discipline issues to the head of school, giving students a chance to grapple with complicated and sometimes-ambiguous violations of the honor code and then having them share the outcomes with the community. This goes a long way toward developing an ownership of the ethical mindset in the student body. If your school does not have an honor or ethics code, what about trying to pilot one in your class? At the surface, this seems to be about behavioral modification, or discipline of students. However, when communities (classes, schools, or districts) take a careful look at determining their core values and then making ways to make them visible in a way that students will believe and care about, then it stands to reason that it will impact decisions about what work they choose to do, and how they do it.

Enable and Encourage Student-Designed Courses of Study (Expanding: Advanced)

Just as doctoral students at universities choose a community of faculty to support their inquiry, what if student-initiated projects in our middle and upper schools were evaluated and supported by a committee of students and teachers? Instead of assuming that students would receive credit in a given department (if the school still has departments and graduation requirements), at the completion of a project, students and faculty can grant credit in departments based on demonstrated learning in the project.

Engage Community Connections (Implementing: Intermediate)

Another possibility is to establish intentional links to the community and organizations or businesses in which the teachers or the school believe that these ethics are exemplified. In communities all over the world, there are people doing work similar to what Nicole is doing in San Pancho. We need to connect our students to these leaders and provide opportunities to learn with them. Cameron Ishee (2014) reflects on the important role that "real professionals" played in her learning about zoos throughout her high school career. At first she was intimidated to call with her questions, but eventually, buoyed by her ethical foundation and deep desire to make change, she stopped thinking of herself as just a high school kid and started feeling her role as a valuable contributing member of the global community of people engaging in this topic. Creating or tapping into a database of community organizations or individuals that are willing to work with, or at least take the occasional call from, our students to consult with them on their projects is a great start. Engaging with community organizations can be simple and short term to complex and long term.

In the School System

Redesign Your Schedule (Expanding: Advanced)

Going even further, schools can explore ways to adjust schedules to give students time and flexibility throughout the days and school year so that they can engage with these people or institutions in meaningful, sustained ways, giving them the opportunity to internalize and reflect on the good work going on in the community. Some schools, like a number of universities, have short terms at some point throughout the year so that students can have access to internships in the "off season." This allows their students to go on consulting and research trips across town or all over the world without having to go through the challenges of "missing school." If schools are able to stop thinking about missing school and start thinking about missing learning, it would be much easier for students to find the opportunities to connect with their passions. And there is no student population or demographic in which this opportunity would not be of tremendous service.

This could be a way for us to determine credits and grades, in which we base them on students' ability to impact change for good, and not just complete a set of pre-established tasks that left them constantly asking "When am I going to use this?"

Honor Students Distinction (Beginning)

Create a way to distinguish and honor students who are achieving social change through their learning. This could be a distinction or seal on their diploma, or a certificate of some sort. Have high standards for what this means in your school system and make sure it is tied to meaningful outcomes and not just hours of service.

Student Governance (Implementing to Advanced)

To demonstrate to students that they are valued individuals and that their voices are heard, give at least half of the seats on important decision-making committees (e.g., school board committees, groups that oversee curriculum and scheduling, etc.) to students. Engage students as peers and not as children.

Support Centers (Advanced)

Create offices or centers that are designed to support student entrepreneurship. Give them office space and legal, intellectual property, and marketing support for student-run and generated concepts, services, and companies.

OVERCOMING CHALLENGES

Trusting Students

If educators bring a distrust of students to their work, it can be a stretch to believe that they can be successful in establishing, understanding, and then acting on the ethical aspirations that we have for them (and hope they have for each other). In this model, teachers have to work to trust students and hold them accountable for their actions by establishing a culture of high accountability and high trust.

As teachers, it can be hard to let go of the reins and let students take control of how and what students learn. With this model, we are suggesting that they not only determine what and how to learn, but they also have a hand in defining the ethical culture in which that learning occurs. This seems big and might seem impossible if we do not believe that students are capable of (in the right environment, with the right support and preparation) making great choices.

Finding Time

This is always a crutch for educators: "But there is no time!" In a classroom or school where student learning is truly personal, there is time. If the time you spend with your students is focused on you communicating predetermined content to them, it's easy to see how there is little time for thoughtful discussions about ethical norms. But if you have a classroom where each student is engaged in his or her own process and inquiry, you can imagine that the work of the whole class (when they are all together) will actually center on these common themes.

What Are Our Values?

This can be a challenge. In what ways does the leadership of your school or district talk about what the values are? In a religious school, this might be clearer; however, even the work of translating religious values into an understandable set of norms for students is the work of all teachers. If your community is lacking a clear and shared sense of values, you should feel empowered to create a sense of ethical behavior and work in your class.

Can Learning Be Evaluated and Measured?

In education, we tend to shy away from the complex noncognitive dimensions of the work we do with students precisely because we cannot measure it easily. As so many have said, just because you can measure something, doesn't mean you should, and just because we don't yet know how to measure something, doesn't mean it has no value in schools. If every educator on earth made a small commitment to nurturing the sense of responsibility that comes with acting on social entrepreneurship, it would be a tremendous shift for the better.

REFLECTION

As eager as educators are for change and opportunities to create a world class learning environment for students, we know it is hard work. Still, when we think about why these efforts are necessary, why we can no longer submit to the status quo in our schools, we realize that we need to push through challenges, questions, assumptions, structures, and conventions on behalf of our students. We demand that our students have the chance to make their learning matter. As educators, it is our commitment to improve the world not just through our students, but for our students. With this strong commitment that our students' learning serve a purpose and improve the world, educators will be able to transform the current paradigm of education into a world class paradigm. These may feel like big shifts, but if we start at the beginning stages and work our way up to the advanced stages, we will be on the road to significant change for the better.

Activity #1: The Distance Between Our Mission and What Our Students Do

Participants

Teachers

Objective

One of the greatest barriers to deeply examining the ethical framework of your school is the distance between mission, values, beliefs, actions. This activity encourages teachers to try to "see" the mission in their students' work. This exercise should help teacher groups begin to break down the barriers about what excellent student work can look like.

Materials

- Small group tables or desks in groups (seat three to four participants)
- Post-it notes
- Markers

Process

This activity can be done in a faculty meeting or a smaller setting with a group of teachers.

Prior to the meeting, send out the following to the teachers:

Thought assignment prior to the meeting: In our next meeting, we will be discussing student work. Please bring one of the following to the meeting with the names of your student redacted:

1. An exceptional piece of student work. This should be a piece of work that you think represents a good learning

experience for the student and a good lesson, assessment, or curricular design on your part.

2. A piece of work where you think the student didn't make the most of the learning.

Step 1: To start the gathering, have people share their student work in groups of four to five participants. (15 minutes)

Each teacher should present the following:

1. Briefly describe the assignment.

2. Describe why you think it was excellent or missed the mark.

Step 2: As a group, fill ten to twenty post-it notes with words that represent the values that come through in the work. What are the skills or knowledge that these assignments or student work represent? Or, you might ask, what is being assessed in this work? Then ask the teachers from all of the groups to put the notes up on one wall. (3 minutes)

Step 3: Next, pass out the mission statement, or vision or academic philosophy, and ask teachers to discuss it at their table and fill another ten to twenty post-it notes per group with words or thoughts that come directly from the mission statement or are implicit in it for the teachers. Then post those words on another wall. (5 minutes):

Step 4: Have the teachers do a "gallery walk" of the two walls and then engage in a large group discussion about the distance between what student work looks like and what the mission of the school is. (10 minutes)

Step 5: If there is time, ask teachers to brainstorm about ways to bridge the gap between the two walls. (5–30 minutes)

- How might student work serve the mission of the school?
- How might student work better represent the mission of social justice and academic excellence?

ACTIVITY #2: RETHINKING RIGOR

Participants

Administrators and/or teachers and students

Objective

A major barrier to creating environments in which students have space to pursue their passions and create meaningful products is a fixed mindset about the definition of rigor.

Materials

- Online chat platform (for a synchronous meeting)
- Small group discussion space

Process

In small groups, or in online discussion spaces, have a conversation about what rigor means at the school. Start by inviting teachers to define rigor in the context of their classes, and then have a subset of the faculty or administrative team synthesize the responses.

- What are the ways that the school can value excellence without being overly reliant on rigor as a characteristic of the learning environment?

Follow this up with small discussion groups with an even mix of faculty and students in the school (for middle school– or high school–age students). Use the following prompts:

- What does "high quality" or "excellence" mean at our school?
- What are the ways in which students have the opportunity to create or do high quality or excellent work that is not teacher directed?
- What is the perception of "projects" at the school?

- What happens at our school when a teacher doesn't know what the end product of a piece of work will look like? How comfortable are we with that as a community?
- If we are uncomfortable about it, what is the relationship between that discomfort and the perception of lower standards and perceived lack of rigor?

ACTIVITY #3: LOOKING AT WHAT OUR GRADUATES DO

Participants

School administrative teams or districts

Objective

This activity will help schools consider the measurement of the value of their product (education) to both the learners and the community as the school chooses to define both value and community.

Process

Conduct a longitudinal look at the alumni of your school. If possible, collect data about the types of fields that students pursue. Select some of your most celebrated graduates who are doing work that the board or administration thinks really exemplifies the kind of impact to global good that the school is striving for.

Then, conduct interviews with these individuals and ask them questions about the following topics:

- What are the kinds of skills that they need to do their work?
- What are the ways that their schooling prepared them for this experience?
- What are the ways in which their experience at the school fell short?

Use the findings to prompt discussion or nudge curricular pilots within the school.

ACTIVITY #4: DISCUSSION PROMPTS FOR SCHOOL BOARDS OR ADMINISTRATIVE TEAMS

Objective

To provoke thinking or provide a way to initiate discussions about curricular change in your school. These discussion prompts will allow school boards or administrative teams to explore the ways to align the mission of the school with the learning experience of the students.

- What (if any) are the moral or philosophical questions that seem to be hard for our community to address?
- How is our governance of the school(s) related to our own experience of school?
- Describe a moment when your experience of school may have impacted how you viewed a new program, initiative, or curriculum.
- What are the things that we think school should "do" for our students?
- Where are the innovation zones in our school(s)?
- What is the tolerance for risk with new ways of teaching and learning?
- How might we emphasize those "innovation zones" to infuse a sense of continual exploration and growth for all the learners in the schools?

REFERENCES

Entreamigos. Retrieved July 7, 2014, from http://entreamigos.org.mx

Ishee, C. (2014, Spring). Education, expanded. *UnBoxed: A Journal of Adult Learning in Schools, 11,* 12–15. Retrieved from http://www.hightechhigh.org/unboxed/issue11/education_expanded/

Kirp, D. L. (2014, August 16). Teaching is not a business. *New York Times*. Retrieved from http://www.nytimes.com/2014/08/17/opinion/sunday/teaching-is-not-a-business.html?smid=fb-share

Santos, F. M. (2012). A positive theory of social entrepreneurship. *Journal of Business Ethics, 111*(3), 335–351. doi:10.1007/s10551-012-1413-4

Weissbourd, R., Jones, S., Anderson, T. R., Kahn, J., & Russell, M. (2014). *The children we mean to raise: The real messages adults are sending about values.* Boston, MA: Harvard Graduate School of Education.

Zhao, Y. (2012). *World class learners: Educating creative and entrepreneurial students.* Thousand Oaks, CA: Corwin.

RESOURCES

Hu, W., & Bromwich, J. (2015, January 29). A boy praises the principal of his Brooklyn school, and a fund-raising campaign takes off. *New York Times*. Retrieved from http://www.nytimes.com/2015/02/01/nyregion/a-boy-praises-the-principal-of-his-brooklyn-school-and-a-fund-raising-campaign-takes-off.html?_r=1

Rosenbaum, S. (2015, February 2). 'Humans of New York' blogger raises over $1M for students. *New York Post*. Retrieved from http://nypost.com/2015/02/02/humans-of-new-york-blogger-raises-over-1m-for-students/

Index

CORWIN
A SAGE Company

Helping educators make the greatest impact

CORWIN HAS ONE MISSION: to enhance education through intentional professional learning.

We build long-term relationships with our authors, educators, clients, and associations who partner with us to develop and continuously improve the best evidence-based practices that establish and support lifelong learning.

Solutions you want. Experts you trust. Results you need.

Author Consulting

Author Consulting

On-site professional learning with sustainable results! Let us help you design a professional learning plan to meet the unique needs of your school or district. www.corwin.com/pd

Institutes

Institutes

Corwin Institutes provide collaborative learning experiences that equip your team with tools and action plans ready for immediate implementation. www.corwin.com/institutes

eCourses

eCourses

Practical, flexible online professional learning designed to let you go at your own pace. www.corwin.com/ecourses

Read2Earn

Read2Earn

Did you know you can earn graduate credit for reading this book? Find out how: www.corwin.com/read2earn

Contact an account manager at (800) 831-6640 or visit **www.corwin.com** for more information.